**New Directions for
Teaching and Learning**

Marilla D. Svinicki
EDITOR-IN-CHIEF

D0707299

The Role of the Classroom in College Student Persistence

John M. Braxton
EDITOR

Number 115 • Fall 2008
Jossey-Bass
San Francisco

THE ROLE OF THE CLASSROOM IN COLLEGE STUDENT PERSISTENCE
John M. Braxton (ed.)
New Directions for Teaching and Learning, no. 115
Marilla D. Svinicki, Editor-in-Chief

Microfilm copies of issues and articles are available in 16mm and 35mm, as well as microfiche in 105mm, through University Microfilms, Inc., 300 North Zeeb Road, Ann Arbor, Michigan 48106-1346.

NEW DIRECTIONS FOR TEACHING AND LEARNING (ISSN 0271-0633, electronic ISSN 1536-0768) is part of The Jossey-Bass Higher and Adult Education Series and is published quarterly by Wiley Subscription Services, Inc., A Wiley Company, at Jossey-Bass, 989 Market Street, San Francisco, California 94103-1741. Periodicals postage paid at San Francisco, California, and at additional mailing offices. POSTMASTER: Send address changes to New Directions for Teaching and Learning, Jossey-Bass, 989 Market Street, San Francisco, California 94103-1741.

New Directions for Teaching and Learning is indexed in CIJE: Current Index to Journals in Education (ERIC), Contents Pages in Education (T&F), Current Abstracts (EBSCO), Educational Research Abstracts Online (T&F), ERIC Database (Education Resources Information Center), Higher Education Abstracts (Claremont Graduate University), and SCOPUS (Elsevier).

SUBSCRIPTIONS cost $89 for individuals and $228 for institutions, agencies, and libraries in the United States. Prices subject to change. See order form at end of book.

EDITORIAL CORRESPONDENCE should be sent to the editor-in-chief, Marilla D. Svinicki, Department of Educational Psychology, University of Texas at Austin, One University Station, D5800, Austin, TX 78712.

www.josseybass.com

CONTENTS

EDITOR'S NOTES

College student departure poses a persistent problem to colleges and universities that attracts the interest of both scholars and practitioners. Approximately 45 percent of students enrolled in two-year colleges depart during their first year, and approximately one out of every fourth student departs from a four-year college or university (American College Testing Program, 2005). These departure rates varied little between 1987 and 2001 (American College Testing Program, 2005). These rates of departure negatively affect the stability of institutional enrollments, budgets, and the public perception of the quality of colleges and universities. Braxton, Sullivan, and Johnson (1997) call this problem the "departure puzzle.

The departure puzzle has been the object of empirical attention for over seventy-five years (Braxton, 2000). During the past thirty years, considerable progress on understanding this puzzle has occurred as Tinto's interactionalist theory of college student departure achieved paradigmatic stature as a framework for understanding college student departure. Its stature is indexed in over 775 citations to his theoretical work (Braxton, Hirschy, and McClendon, 2004). Nevertheless, based on their assessment of empirical support for the propositions of Tinto's interactionalist theory, Braxton, Sullivan, and Johnson (1997) conclude that this theory receives partial support in residential colleges and universities and little or no backing in commuter colleges and universities. As a consequence, in *Understanding and Reducing College Student Departure* (2004), Braxton, Hirschy, and McClendon advance a serious revision of Tinto's theory for residential colleges and universities and a new theory for commuter colleges and universities. Alan Seidman's edited book, *College Student Retention: Formula for Student Success* (2005), provides an additional treatment of aspects pertinent to our knowledge and understanding of student departure such as the measurement of persistence, definitions of retention, reliable knowledge about student departure, degree attainment, and the role of finances.

Despite such advances in our understanding of student departure, much work remains to be done on the translation of theory and research into practice (Tinto, 2006). Tinto puts this need into sharp focus by stating, "Unfortunately, most institutions have not yet been able to translate what we know about student retention into forms of action that have led to substantial gains in student persistence and graduation" (2006, p. 5). Such a translation of theory and research into practice requires a scholarship of practice. Eraut (1988) identifies four types of knowledge needed for professional practice. Of these four types, applicatory knowledge, which

NEW DIRECTIONS FOR TEACHING AND LEARNING, no. 115, Fall 2008 © Wiley Periodicals, Inc.
Published online in Wiley InterScience (www.interscience.wiley.com) • DOI: 10.1002/tl.321

1

involves the translation of technical knowledge into prescriptions for action, best fits the type of knowledge Tinto urges.

Tinto (2006) identifies the classroom as fertile ground for the translation of theory and research into practice. Empirical research focused on the relationship between classroom practices and student persistence constitutes a critical step in such a translation. Braxton, Hirschy, and McClendon (2004) also posit a significant role for the classroom in student persistence in both residential and commuter colleges and universities.

Curricular structure and pedagogical practice shape the role the classroom plays in student persistence (Tinto, 1997, 2000). Some research demonstrates this role (Nora, Cabrera, Hagedorn, and Pascarella, 1996; Tinto, 1997; Braxton, Bray, and Berger, 2000; and Braxton, Milem, and Sullivan, 2000). Despite this growing recognition of the role the classroom plays in student persistence, the communities of research and practice need more empirical work to guide the translation of research into practices designed to reduce institutional rates of student departure. The *New Directions for Teaching and Learning* series provides an optimum medium for the presentation of such empirical work because of its role as a nexus between these two communities. This volume intends to serve such a purpose.

The chapters of this volume bring into sharp focus the complexity of the role that college and university faculty members play in shaping the persistence and departure decisions of undergraduate college students. Unfortunately, faculty members do not view student retention as their responsibility (Tinto, 2006). Nevertheless, they need to acknowledge the role they play in student persistence or departure decisions. Given that academics are likely to respond to empirical evidence about their role, the research findings presented in the chapters that follow should give faculty members some of the evidence they need to acknowledge the part they play in student persistence.

The empirical work included in this volume ranges from curricular structures and instructional staffing policies to the teaching practices of college and university faculty members. This volume consists of seven chapters, and each offers recommendations for institutional practice.

Curricular structures include learning communities: groups of students who take the same courses together, sometimes with an underlying theme to these courses (Tinto, 1997). Although empirical work on learning communities exists (Tinto, 1997; Zhao and Kuh, 2004), Cathy McHugh Engstrom focuses in Chapter One on the role of learning communities in promoting the persistence of underprepared college students. Learning communities give rise to pedagogical practices. Engstrom describes four teaching practices faculty use in teaching in learning communities that serve underprepared students. In Chapter Two, Jillian Kinzie, Robert Gonyea, Rick Shoup, and George D. Kuh also devote some attention to curricular policies and classroom practices that benefit underrepresented students enrolled in institutions of higher education. They derived their findings from the Connecting the Dots project that used a combination of academic transcript data and responses to the National Survey of Student Engagement made by sixty-two hundred students at eighteen colleges and universities that include four historically black colleges and universities and three Hispanic-serving institutions.

Another aspect of the role of the classroom in college student persistence pertains to the instructional staffing of courses. The staffing of courses by contingent faculty in general and part-time faculty in particular looms particularly important given the findings of Ehrenberg and Zhang (2005) that increasing the number of part-time faculty has a negative impact on student graduation rates. In Chapter Three, M. Kevin Eagan Jr. and Audrey J. Jaeger give empirical attention to the effects of the proportion of graduate students and part-time faculty teaching gatekeeper courses on first-year student persistence. In their study, Eagan and Jaeger define gatekeeper courses as introductory courses in the fields of chemistry, biology, physics, mathematics, engineering, economics, sociology, and psychology.

Teaching skills and teaching practices of college and university faculty members form additional aspects of the college classroom that play a role in college student persistence. Chapters Four through Six present the findings of empirical treatments of these classroom aspects. In Chapter Four, Ernest T. Pascarella, Tricia A. Seifert, and Elizabeth J. Whitt address the influence of such faculty teaching skills as organization and preparation and clarity in instruction and answering student questions on first-year student persistence. In Chapter Five, John M. Braxton, Willis A. Jones, Amy S. Hirschy, and Harold V. Hartley III address the part that active learning plays in first-year student persistence. In Chapter Six, Thomas F. Nelson Laird, Daniel Chen, and George D. Kuh compare faculty teaching practices at colleges and universities with better-than-expected persistence rates with those at colleges and universities with as-expected persistence rates. In addition to teaching practices, they concentrate on the emphasis faculty give to intellectual and practical skills as course outcomes.

In Chapter Seven, I put forth the elements of a scholarship of practice centered on improving institutional rates of college student retention. In formulating these elements, I identify three contributions to a scholarship of practice made by the chapter authors. I also offer four recommendations for institutional policy and action designed to improve institutional rates of student retention.

College and university presidents, chief academic affairs officers, academic deans, directors and staff members of campus-based centers for teaching, and individuals responsible for enrollment management will find the contents of this volume useful to their practice. Scholars of faculty role performance will also find the contents of this volume useful to their research, as will scholars of college student retention.

College student retention remains a nettlesome problem confronting individual colleges and universities. By focusing on the role of the classroom, this volume demonstrates the feasibility of a scholarship of practice centered on improving institutional rates of student retention. Through a scholarship of practice centered on the classroom and other dimensions of colleges and universities, some headway on increasing the rates of student retention at individual colleges and universities may prove possible.

John M. Braxton
Editor

References

American College Testing Program. *National Collegiate Retention and Persistence to Degree Rates.* Iowa City, Ia., 2005.

Braxton, J. M. "Introduction: Reworking the Student Departure Puzzle." In J. M. Braxton (ed.), *Reworking the Student Departure Puzzle.* Nashville, Tenn.: Vanderbilt University Press, 2000.

Braxton, J. M., Bray, N. J., and Berger, J. B. "Faculty Teaching Skills and Their Influence on the College Student Departure Process." *Journal of College Student Development,* 2000, *41,* 215–227.

Braxton, J. M., Hirschy, A. S., and McClendon, S. A. *Understanding and Reducing College Student Departure.* ASHE-ERIC Higher Education Report, vol. 30, no. 3. San Francisco: Jossey-Bass, 2004.

Braxton, J. M., Milem, J. F., and Sullivan, A. S. "The Influence of Active Learning on the College Student Departure Process." *Journal of Higher Education,* 2000, *71,* 569–590.

Braxton, J. M., Sullivan, A. S., and Johnson, R. M. "Appraising Tinto's Theory of College Student Departure." In J. C. Smart (ed.), *Higher Education: Handbook of Theory and Research.* New York: Agathon Press, 1997.

Ehrenberg, R. G., and Zhang, L. "Do Tenure and Tenure-Track Faculty Matter?" *Journal of Human Resources,* 2005, *40,* 647–659.

Eraut, M. "Knowledge Creation and Knowledge Use in Professional Contexts." *Studies in Higher Education,* 1988, *10,* 117–132.

Nora, A., Cabrera, A., Hagedorn, L., and Pascarella, E. "Differential Impacts of Academic and Social Experiences on College-Related Behavioral Outcomes Across Different Ethnic and Gender Groups at Four-Year Institutions." *Research in Higher Education,* 1996, *37,* 427–451.

Seidman, A. (ed.). *College Student Retention: Formula for Success.* Westport, Conn.: American Council on Higher Education/Praeger, 2005.

Tinto, V. "Classrooms as Communities: Exploring the Educational Character of Student Persistence." *Journal of Higher Education,* 1997, *68,* 599–623.

Tinto, V. "Linking Learning and Leaving: Exploring the Role of the College Classroom in Student Departure." In J. M. Braxton (ed.), *Reworking the Student Departure Puzzle.* Nashville, Tenn.: Vanderbilt University Press, 2000.

Tinto, V. "Research and Practice of Student Retention: What Next?" *Journal of College Student Retention,* 2006, *8,* 1–19.

Zhao, C., and Kuh, G. "Adding Value: Learning Communities and Student Engagement." *Research in Higher Education,* 2004, *45,* 115–136.

JOHN M. BRAXTON is professor of education in the Higher Education Leadership and Policy Program at Peabody College, Vanderbilt University, in Nashville, Tennessee.

NEW DIRECTIONS FOR TEACHING AND LEARNING • DOI: 10.1002/tl

1

This chapter describes the key role of faculty in creating active, integrative learning experiences for students in basic skills learning communities, providing forums for students to extend time on task, and validating that students both belong and will be successful in college.

Curricular Learning Communities and Unprepared Students: How Faculty Can Provide a Foundation for Success

Cathy McHugh Engstrom

Over forty years ago, Patricia Cross asserted that higher education must "democratize" its colleges and universities (1971, p. 4). Since that time, institutions have enrolled more students from diverse backgrounds, particularly in terms of race/ethnicity, national origin, and age. The number of students attending colleges and universities has increased over 25 percent in the past twenty years. As overall enrollments have grown, so have the number of economically disadvantaged students who attend college (National Center for Education Statistics, 2005). The number of students of color attending American colleges has nearly doubled, from 15 to 28 percent (Lamkin, 2004). Daunting challenges still remain to improve the completion of baccalaureate degrees, particularly for those who come unprepared. As Cross claimed in the early 1970s, it is not enough to enroll these "new" students. She realized that if higher education did not make educational programs fit diverse student learning styles, needs, and educational backgrounds, these students would fail.

Typically institutions did not change their educational systems or practices. As a result, despite recent gains in access to college, especially among some underrepresented racial/ethnic groups, similar increases in rates of

Funding for this research project was provided by the Lumina Foundation for Education and the William and Flora Hewlett Foundation. The coinvestigators for the overall project were Vincent Tinto and Cathy McHugh Engstrom.

college graduation have not occurred (American Council on Education, 2001). This decline occurred during a period when much attention has been paid to developmental education and academic support in both two- and four-year colleges and universities. Our society still struggles with translating gains in access to college into increases in college completion.

Clearly the importance of understanding how faculty can promote student success for unprepared students is more pressing than ever before. The challenge is particularly great in the urban two- and four-year colleges that serve large numbers of working-class and underrepresented students. In those institutions, it is estimated that approximately 45 percent of beginning students participate in some form of academic support or basic skills courses (National Center for Education Statistics, 1997). These figures may underestimate the need for academic assistance since more students in those institutions who require developmental assistance do not receive it (Boylan, 1999; Boylan and Saxon, 1999).

Typically these students are required to complete one or more non-credit-bearing courses in reading, writing, or mathematics, or some combination of these. By the 1990s, almost one-third of all students were placed in basic skills or developmental classes in their first year: 42 percent in two-year public colleges and 20 percent in four-year public institutions (National Center for Education Statistics, 2003). Community colleges play a central role in providing these courses; over 60 percent of first-year students are enrolled in these courses. For example, in California, 75 percent of community college students are identified as not ready for college-level math or English (Burdman, 2006). Unprepared students are not unique to students enrolled in community colleges. Among entering freshmen in 1998 in the California state system (baccalaureate- and master's-granting institutions), just less than two-thirds of students failed the math placement test and 43 percent failed the verbal test. In addition, 42 percent of faculty across all types of higher education institutions reported that most of their students lack the basic skills necessary to succeed in college-level work (Lindholm, Szelenyi, Hurtado, and Korn, 2005). With over $1 billion a year being spent on basic skills programs, many policymakers are critical of these practices and crying for evidence of the role or effects of basic skills classes on student outcomes such as grade point average, persistence, and other indicators of student success (Bettinger and Long, 2003).

Students may be unprepared for a variety of reasons, such as inadequate schooling experiences, competing family and work demands, lack of English language competency, or unfamiliarity with how college works. These are disproportionately students of color, first-generation college goers, from working-class families, with English not their primary language; they often are required to work part or full time with reduced academic loads (Smith, MacGregor, Matthews, and Gabelnick, 2004).

Many urban two- and four-year colleges are ill prepared to deal with the substantial developmental needs that students bring to the classroom.

NEW DIRECTIONS FOR TEACHING AND LEARNING • DOI: 10.1002/tl

Often these colleges have not been complacent in their efforts; they have dedicated a substantial proportion of their resources to basic skills course work for unprepared students. Unfortunately, these courses have been delivered in traditional, nonengaging, even alienating ways. In typical basic skills courses, students are in classes requiring monotonous "sentence completion exercise, arithmetic drills, and three paragraph essays on contrived topics" (Grubb and Associates, 1999, p. 204). It is not surprising that students are withdrawing at high rates from these classes and leaving college.

The classroom is one key arena, if not the only one available, for unprepared students to participate in powerful, meaningful learning opportunities. More attention is now being paid to restructuring how classrooms or courses are organized and taught to meet students' diverse learning needs; engage them in an integrated rather than a fragmented, disconnected curriculum; and build foundational skills for college student success. One particularly promising effort is the adaptation of curricular learning communities to the needs of academically underprepared students (Malnarich and others, 2003). Smith, MacGregor, Matthews, and Gabelnick (2004) contended that students taking basic skills or English as a Second Language classes integrated into learning community models can "transform the revolving door into an open door for both access and excellence" (p. 189). The pedagogical assumptions and teaching practices of learning community models reflect exemplary conditions for learning, so using these models with unprepared students seems desirable and worthy of investigation.

Curricular learning communities are not new. They began almost eighty years ago with Meiklejohn's Experimental College at the University of Wisconsin, Madison (Nelson, 2001). Over the past two decades, learning communities have been adopted with varying degrees of success in several hundred four- and two-year colleges (Gablenick, MacGregor, Matthews, and Smith, 1990). Interest in curricular learning communities and the collaborative pedagogy that underlies these models emerges in part from compelling evidence about the importance of involvement in promoting student success. Engagement with others, in particular through active learning activities, provides a variety of positive outcomes that lead to student learning and persistence (Astin, 1993; Cabrera and others, 1998; Carini, Kuh, and Klein, 2006; McKlenney and Greene, 2005; Pascarella and Terenzini, 2005; Tinto, 1993). Several foundations and educational organizations have cited these pedagogical models as one effective practice that improves student engagement (Zhao and Kuh, 2004), learning, and persistence. However, the use of these models with unprepared students has been more limited, and research examining their effectiveness has typically been conducted at a single institution (Engstrom and Tinto, 2006).

Learning communities, in their most basic form, intentionally cluster two or more courses taken by a cohort of students, typically around an interdisciplinary theme. Great diversity in the type of structures and models possible exists, requiring different levels of faculty and student engagement, faculty collaboration, and restructuring of students' (and faculty) time, credit, and activities (Smith, MacGregor, Matthews, and Gabelnick, 2004).

This chapter describes the key role of faculty in creating active, integrative learning experiences for students in basic skills learning communities, providing forums for students to extend time on task, and validating that students both belong and will be successful in college. Information for this chapter came primarily from analyzing over three hundred interviews conducted one or two times a year with students enrolled at one of three community colleges— Cerritos College (Los Angeles, California), DeAnza College (northern California), or Cerritos College (Los Angeles)—or at one four-year institution— California State University-East Bay. Over the course of the study, we interviewed 182 students from these three institutions, some several times. Forty-six students participated in three or more interviews over four years. The themes presented in this chapter around issues of how students experienced the role of faculty in promoting their college success emerged from the data during qualitative analysis (Bodgan and Biklen, 1998; Strauss and Corbin, 1990).

Students in the study had enrolled in a curricular learning community (LC) course that included one or more noncredit-bearing basic skills courses (for example, math, reading, writing, English as a Second Language) linked to another basic skills course or a general education course, or both. These learning communities shared the following characteristics:

- A variety of well-established course offerings and models were offered.
- The courses involved interdisciplinary, team-taught, collaborative learning perspectives and practices.
- First-generation and working-class students from diverse backgrounds, particularly in terms of race/ethnicity/socioeconomic status/national origin, were well represented in the courses.
- Ongoing faculty development was provided for those involved in learning community initiatives.

Most students in these integrated courses did not speak English as their primary language, and many were immigrants from Eastern Europe, Central America, Asia, and Africa. A key component of the interviews examined faculty contributions to their learning.

Whether students were participating in a learning community that linked ESL writing and a credit-bearing history course (DeAnza), a reading/writing-linked course (LART), a house that linked a basic skills math, writing, and counseling and advising seminar (Cerritos), a business academy (LaGuardia), or a quarter-long cluster (CSEB), the findings of this study argue that faculty teaching practices created trusting, safe learning environments that promoted student persistence and success. (I will use the designations in parentheses in this paragraph in the balance of the chapter to identify the course and section in which the student was enrolled.) Other

NEW DIRECTIONS FOR TEACHING AND LEARNING • DOI: 10.1002/tl

pieces of research offer support to this assertion (Braxton, Milem, and Sullivan, 2000; Tinto, 1997).

Faculty Matter: Agents for Building a Positive, Safe Learning Environment

> Like back in high school, I'm not so, how do you say it, I didn't participate, I didn't raise my hand and like speak my mind, and like right now, I do and I do it really often because I feel like I have a voice and I can like share then without like, how do I say it, people looking down on me. 'Cause like in college, it's different. Your opinion . . . you're not judged. That's right. That's what I'm trying to say. You're not judged by others, your classmates, your teachers. (Jasmine)

Jasmine's comments are vivid reminders that many students today enter college not feeling as if the classroom is a safe place to learn. For native English-speaking students, prior high school experiences seemed irrelevant and left them feeling disconnected, invalidated as knowers, and lacking motivation to learn or excel. They consistently voiced that high school was a waste of time; they learned little from the lecture mode of class delivery and spent few hours (if at all) studying. For recent immigrant or nonnative-English-speaking students, their lack of confidence in their academic abilities, self-esteem, and identity as college students was directly tied to their ability to speak, read, and write English.

Students in the various learning community programs indicated that they learned better in these classes. These courses felt different from other stand-alone classes or prior schooling experiences. The conditions for learning did not just happen because students moved from one class to another. Faculty contributed in four interrelated ways to create these safe, engaging learning environments:

- *Active learning pedagogies.* Through the use of active learning pedagogies, faculty created vehicles for students to get to know each other and develop respect and trust, leading to students' increased comfort in participating in a community of learners.
- *Faculty collaboration and an integrative curriculum.* Faculty worked together to develop curricular links between courses. Students perceive these integrated experiences to foster deeper learning, student engagement, fluid teacher-learning roles, and more efficient use of their time.
- *Development of college learning strategies.* Faculty introduced structured opportunities and even incentives for students to learn the skills, habits, and competencies critical to navigating college and promoting ongoing academic success.
- *Student validation.* Faculty validated students through their high expectations, recognition of students' expertise and knowledge, and their

NEW DIRECTIONS FOR TEACHING AND LEARNING • DOI: 10.1002/tl

continued assurance that students were able to do college work. They made students feel welcome and that they belonged in college.

Student interview comments provide vivid snapshots of how faculty created these ripe conditions for learning and offer guidance and concrete suggestions for faculty to better foster student learning, success, and ultimately persistence.

Active Learning Pedagogies

The LC structure and faculty pedagogical practices encouraged students to get to know each other. Students felt comfortable in these classes; faculty and peers encouraged their participation and validated their views. These feelings were prerequisites to participating and learning in and out of class. Faculty's use of group work and activities was effective in fostering student engagement. For example, Jasmine, a black student from Sweden (DeAnza), reflected on the importance of group work to facilitate her comfort level to participate in class:

> I remember sitting in my English class for LART [the reading/writing-linked course] three years ago. I didn't know anybody at all. I didn't know what to expect, and one thing that my teachers taught me very early is to value knowledge and don't be afraid to speak. They were very interested to hear my opinions, what I had to bring, and at that time I was, I wasn't used to it that much. So I was very hesitant, but you know, as the year passed by, as the quarter passed by, I noticed that it's very important to just speak up and hear other people's opinions.

Jane (DeAnza) equated active learning as evidence that faculty cared about her:

> Faculty care more. . . . In the other two classes, the teachers just lecture. They are talking heads. . . . In the learning community, there is a lot more participation, conversation back and forth, and discussion about what we are doing.

Attila (DeAnza) illustrated some concrete strategies LC faculty employed that challenged students to engage in and actively work to understand the material in class:

> Instead of them making a point, like read a story or an essay, they don't just tell you the point of the essay. They start asking questions, and they make you think and find out on your own, but with your classmates. They are not going to say to you, "This is the point of this class," you know, like a lecture class: "This is how you have to do it." No, they are going to make you work for it; you have to find out.

NEW DIRECTIONS FOR TEACHING AND LEARNING • DOI: 10.1002/tl

For many students, faculty efforts to get students talking and learning from one another were new experiences. Sophie (DeAnza) explained:

> The LART classes are really different from what I am used to. I'm not really a person who is interactive in class, but this is totally different compared to past experiences in school. Here, in the circles we form, we hear more from students than the teachers, and I have never done anything like that before. I used to be pretty shy talking in front of people, and it has helped me get used to that and to be more open about participating.

Sue (DeAnza) concurred: "In this environment you become more confident, you become more alive, you become more responsible for your own opinions and you aren't afraid to speak your views, you aren't afraid to speak up." Finally, Elin (DeAnza) explained, "It just is a little different in LART. The teachers give you more examples, they teach a little more and get more people involved by getting people to talk with people. For example, when we did essays, we get into little groups, do peer edits, people reading other people's papers and feeling comfortable to give real feedback."

Clearly faculty recognized beneficial assignments and activities to make learning a public, shared experience. They did not just assign students to groups; they were intentional about introducing activities that got students to know one another, gave them relevant and meaningful issues to discuss, and to teach and learn from one another. Juan (Cerritos) emphasized, "You really don't know something unless you teach it. So like most people, sometimes they don't understand it so if I teach it to them, I'll understand it even better." Jasmine (Cerritos) added:

> We all listen to each other, and we're not afraid to like make the suggestions. It all happens 'cause the teachers helped us know each other and open up to each other. When I first was coming to school, I was like, oh, I'm going to fail 'cause I haven't been in school forever, but now it's been good. I'm not afraid to ask anybody for help or what do you think about this.

Clearly the active learning pedagogy the instructors in these various learning community models employed fostered the friendships described. These relationships became central vehicles for learning and immersed students in an academic environment where they engaged one another.

Another concrete strategy faculty employed to engage students was to connect the course content to the lives of faculty or students. Students learned when they thought the curriculum was relevant to real-life issues, as Lalonnie (CSUEB) shared:

> This cluster is really interesting because most of the books we are reading and things we talk about in class are so real. This cluster gives me solutions to some of the problems that we're going through nowadays. Here we are at

eight o'clock in the morning, all raising our hands to talk. We are talking about important things that go on in life, and everyone always has something to say about it. Learning about all this is really interesting.

Later, students continued to seek connections between the course content and their personal lives, even without faculty encouragement. Elizabeth (Cerritos) explained:

> Since I was in Math 20 with a learning community, it helped because I remember back then, the teachers, they would say that you know math is just solving problems and it's about what you know; try to relate it to your daily life, and you are going to find math everywhere. So that's one of the things I still have with me. I try to make those connections in class if the teacher won't do it for us.

Students' perspectives emphasize that students taking basic skills classes value and are more deeply involved when faculty introduce meaningful group work, push the students to work with the course material as opposed to just digesting information, and make connections to students' own experiences. As the result of group work and time dedicated to help students and faculty to get to know one another, students developed a sense of community or family. This atmosphere created ripe conditions for learning. For example, Issac, who participated in a DeAnza LART (language arts), shared that "one of our students compared this class as more of a family, a small family. . . . It's a closely knit classroom. . . . We were really able to share experiences, and I think it improved me a lot."

Students' views highlight the emotional dimension involved in learning. Learning is scary, and it requires risks (especially to talk) and confidence. ESL students, in particular, are quite anxious and resistant to participate in class until they feel they have become more proficient in the reading, writing, and speaking of the English language. Active learning pedagogies are powerful vehicles to support students' vulnerabilities and build their confidence. The learning communities at the institutions studied clearly were successful in developing safe, meaningful, engaging learning environments in which students felt validated and capable of succeeding in class. Students felt that they belonged to a community of learners.

Faculty Collaboration and Integrative Learning Experiences

LC faculty worked together to link the course content and coordinate assignments and activities so they complemented and built on each other. Stephen (DeAnza) vividly explained how faculty created a curriculum that grew like a puzzle: "Every day, they give us piece by piece, and by the end it all connects together. The teachers have us figure out how to put it together. You have time to focus and absorb everything. The teachers take turns and build on each other's topics, and then we get a deeper understanding of everything." Students said that the courses linked the curriculum, and coordinated assignments led to deeper learning experiences, increased engagement with the course material, and motivation to learn, and faculty and students moved seamlessly back and forth between teacher and learner roles. Finally students claimed that learning in an integrated fashion was easier and more efficient.

Vera (CSUEB) shared an example from her Healthy Living Cluster about ways in which curricular integration led to richer, deeper learning experiences:

> In our GS class, we had to do a presentation about subjects we were learning in chemistry. So I learned the subject matter better in chemistry in getting ready for the speech. Then my English teacher had us write an essay about the significance of chemistry. We had to persuade students to take chemistry—how it's necessary and important in everyday life. So in all this, you're developing your writing skills, your speech skills, and you are learning chemistry. It's like you are developing different skills, but you are learning the same thing in a deeper way.

An ESL student (LaGuardia) taking a linked accounting and ESL writing course highlighted that "the relationship in classes between accounting and ESL is helping a lot because the accounting professor is teaching us to answer questions in complete sentences—to write better. And we are more motivated to learn vocabulary because it is accounting vocabulary—something we want to learn about. I am learning accounting better by learning the accounting language." Kauli (CSEB) shared her excitement that came from better understanding of her class material: "You're working on reading in one class, which totally helps you in your writing class. Everything works together, and I think you're building your skills so much faster because you're being able to compare it. One day you are seeing this, and the other day you are seeing that, and you say, 'Yes! That goes together.'" Gina (CSUEB) added that these links increased her interest level in the subject matter: "At first it all seemed like a lot of information, but because they all connected, it worked really well, so you don't just get one topic and get bored after all. Instead, you get three different topics connecting into one bigger one. It's more interesting."

Faculty's efforts at working collaboratively with other teachers also fostered an environment in which teacher and learner roles were fluid. The students appreciated and provided concrete descriptions of teachers who worked together to make the curricular links that enhanced both their learning and relationships with faculty. Jack (DeAnza) described this process in his learning community:

> Not only does one teacher go over that material, but the next day, the other teacher that I have in that same class will review that and it's intertwined that

way, and the teachers work together as well. They know what has been taught the day before and what they need to go over. Also, one teacher will grade our essay; then she'll hand it off to the next teacher. You see there are notes on either side of the paper—one on the left side and one on the right side. It's cool not just to get one perspective but two. It improves your writing so much more.

John (DeAnza) highlighted the different roles assumed by faculty that enabled teachers at times to learn alongside the students:

What's nice also is that they'll sometimes sit in each other's class. That I found was very cool. Because then you really saw the classes were linked because the other teacher would sit in on the other teacher's class on her off day, and she would not sit there as a teacher; she would sit there as a student. She would take the opportunity to learn. . . . So it made for a nice learning atmosphere. And vice versa, the other teacher would then sit in the other's class, and it wasn't like we had two teachers at that time; one of the teachers was a student with us.

Students valued observing faculty moving from fluid teacher-learner roles. This modeling sent messages to students that they too can move from expert to learner depending on their own knowledge and expertise. In addition, teachers who took on the student or learner mode sent a powerful message to students that it is okay to ask questions, seek out understanding, take risks, ask for clarification, and not know the answer. These behaviors contributed to creating an environment safe and comfortable to learn.

Steve (DeAnza) noted the fluidity of integrated reading-writing classes:

It doesn't feel like you're taking two completely off-the-wall classes. You learn to become a well-rounded reader and writer at the same time. And I don't think, you think you'd get that from the other classes, but I don't think it flows as smoothly as our class does thanks to how the teachers work together. For example, Julie [instructor], she'd say, "Okay, we're going to stop here and you're going to be doing a little more of this with Nicole [instructor]." So she'll, they know, they pretty much know each other's curriculum, like what they're doing, so they'll try to see where they can connect to transition over to each other and make it smooth, which was nice.

Students also found these integrated experiences were fun, convenient, easy, and efficient. Stan (DeAnza) explained, "They try and they try and lessen our work load by conjoining both classes together, so usually one class will relate to the other one instead of dividing it into separate classes where we read two different books. We read the same book and do the same work for both classes."

Due to the efforts of faculty working together and identifying curricular links, students described learning as more relevant, interesting, fun,

NEW DIRECTIONS FOR TEACHING AND LEARNING • DOI: 10.1002/tl

deep, and "better." Students said that these integrated experiences were more efficient, easier, and fostered more understanding and comprehension. They enjoyed watching peers, faculty, and themselves shifting from experts to learners depending on the situation. To observe their faculty assume the learner or student role, they shared a collective openness and vulnerability to learn together. These experiences shaped their future efforts to find similar connections and coherence in their course work.

Increasing Time on Task: Promoting Study Groups, Tutoring, and Other Support Services

In these learning community courses, faculty carved out time in their classes to encourage students to form study groups, access tutoring services, and seek out academic support offices. These activities became integrated into students' weekly schedules and routines, even after the learning community experience ended. It was not unusual for students to have a study group and one or more tutoring sessions each week. Faculty steadily encouraged students to set up and participate in study groups. These activities engaged students in college pursuits, they spent more hours studying, and they were serious about their studies. Max (DeAnza) explained: "We motivate each other, and we keep each other on track. Cherry and I are in these classes together, so we usually are doing our homework together. We have discussions with ourselves—sometimes heated discussions on a lot of different topics. When we get back to class, we know what we want to talk about, ask about, what we want to present. So it helps to have friends to help you with essays, readings, discussion topics." Faculty efforts to push classroom learning outside the class assisted students in being better prepared when they returned to class.

Most students had never participated or even considered these forums for studying in high school. It was not enough for students to be encouraged to participate in study groups. Faculty took an active role in teaching them how to set up and facilitate these forums. For example, faculty at Cal State East Bay emphasized forming study groups and introduced structures and motivations for students to do so. In one GS class, before an exam was to occur in one of the linked LC classes, the professor put the study group assignments up on the board and discussed ways in which the study group members should work together to prepare for the exam. Students did not leave the class until they had their group and had set aside time to meet. Other faculty offered extra credit for study group participation. Anna (CSUEB) explained how faculty used BlackBoard to organize study groups: "They told us to have an open bulletin board on BlackBoard like 'study group at this time during class' and everyone is more than welcome to join."

Allison (CSEB) shared some concrete ways in which she benefited from study groups:

> I have study groups—in my remedial English class where we actually get together and write papers together or research topics together. And I actually, I have them all in my English class now, and I have them all in sociology with me. We will just get together out of knowing each other now, and, "Okay, I have to write this paper; let's go to the library," or, "I haven't had library class yet. Have you had it yet? We'll teach you how to use it."

Study groups enabled students to learn material more thoroughly and stay focused and engaged in their academic work. These students faced endless work, family responsibilities, and other distractions in their lives. The study group provided an excuse to stay on campus longer, to be immersed and not distracted from their academics, and to study in a fun, productive, stimulating environment.

Faculty also used class time to encourage students to use tutors and other campus supports. They invited academic advisers (counselors) in on a regular basis to talk about their services or just to join in and participate in class activities. They transformed their class into a web of integrated activities that extend into the campus community.

Faculty Validation

Faculty validation came in many forms and was deeply integrated into instructors' day-to-day teaching practices. Faculty passion about their teaching, student success, and high expectations for performance motivated students to work hard and persist through challenging moments. Faculty members who knew their students well and served as their ongoing cheerleaders and advocates contributed to students' increased confidence and motivation to succeed in college. Danielle at Cerritos emphasized that the passion of her teachers motivated her to learn: "Our teachers are so passionate about what they are doing. . . . It is much more fun, interesting, and motivational for us as a student to meet a teacher that cares." Nemo (DeAnza) had similar views of the importance of faculty who demonstrated excitement about their work: "The teacher . . . she was always positive. And I just, it amazed me. I said, 'Where does she get her enthusiasm?' You know, every day it's the same, so I guess it's just a drive, a love of how students learn to grow, to prosper."

Teachers not only motivated students to get engaged through their positive outlook and energy but also served as invaluable advocates or cheerleaders for students. These groups of students have not experienced many teachers who have believed in their academic capabilities. Consequently faculty validation of their abilities is particularly powerful and meaningful to students. Jasmine (DeAnza) voiced how she felt about that first-quarter LART Writing course and the instructor's role: "In the beginning, I was not confident in my writing, but you know, she came up to me and said, 'You know, I don't want you to be discouraged. I am here to help you, and when you see the results later on, you'll realize that, okay, you know, I can do

NEW DIRECTIONS FOR TEACHING AND LEARNING • DOI: 10.1002/tl

this!'" Roberto (Cerritos) explained that one teacher spent time in each class to validate students' anxieties while also affirming her belief in them: "The instructors really relate to us. Their message to us is always positive. Always. It's, 'You can do it. Hang in there. Don't give up.' They go out of their way to say you can succeed. 'Come see me if you have problem.'" Lucinda (Cerritos) added, ". . . They made you feel good for what you are doing. They made you just want to keep coming to school." Faculty recognized the risks associated with student learning, the struggles and insecurities that students faced; they did not take for granted the importance of repeating over and over their confidence in students' abilities.

Recommendations and Conclusions

Students in this study highlighted critical conditions that faculty created to foster student success. They valued faculty efforts to organize and implement integrative learning experiences characterized by active learning strategies, assignments, and activities that encouraged learning to continue outside the classroom (for example, in study groups), and validation of students' abilities and a sense of belonging in both class and college as a whole. The learning community models introduced structures for faculty to more easily promote these teaching practices. The learning community models encouraged faculty communication and cooperation to link course content and assignments. The structures made instructors' teaching more public and shared, so feedback about teaching effectiveness became immediate and transparent. Teachers moved back and forth from teacher-learner roles. Students who just a few months earlier had described themselves as passive, uninvolved, disinterested high school students were now engaged in relevant, caring learning environments. Teacher practices were at the heart of these changing conditions.

Institutions serious about supporting the academic success and persistence of underprepared students must prepare their teachers, not just the students, about what these students need to learn and succeed. Faculty development efforts must be targeted to restructuring how we deliver instruction and using the classroom to integrate academic support services. These students are easily distracted and often wrestling with competing demands that will pull them away from the classroom. As a result, faculty must use their classes to introduce and teach them the benefits of extending their learning with peers and other campus supports. They want to teach students that these activities are part of the course experience and not add-ons or extras. Faculty might be the only conduit for students to direct them to these services. Finally, teaching content effectively is not sufficient. Faculty must also convince students that they care about and believe in them and that students' academic success matters. The affective dimensions of learning and student progress must be an ongoing dimension of the teaching process. These practices are central to laying the foundation for the first-year success of a group of students who are often struggling to learn and persist.

References

American Council on Education. *Annual Status Report on Minorities in Higher Education.* Washington D.C.: American Council on Education, 2001.

Astin, A. *What Matters in College.* San Francisco: Jossey-Bass, 1993.

Bettinger, E., and Long, B. *The Role and Effect of Remedial Education in Two-Year Colleges.* Ithaca, N.Y.: Cornell Higher Education Institute, 2003.

Boylan, H. "Exploring Alternatives to Remediation." *Journal of Developmental Education,* 1999, 22(3), 2–8.

Boylan, H., and Saxon, D. P. "Remedial Courses: Estimates of Student Participation and the Volume of Remediation in U.S. Community Colleges." Unpublished manuscript, 1999.

Braxton, J. M., Milem, J. F., and Sullivan, A. S. "The Influence of Active Learning on the College Student Departure Process: Toward a Revision of Tinto's Theory." *Journal of Higher Education,* 2000, 71, 569–590.

Burdman, P. *California Community Colleges Focus Area. Draft.* Palo Alto, Calif.: William and Flora Hewlett Foundation Education Program, 2006.

Cabrera, A. F., and others. "Collaborative Learning: Preferences, Gains in Cognitive and Affective Outcomes, and Openness to Diversity Among College Students." Paper presented at the annual meeting of the Association for the Study of Higher Education, Miami, Fla., 1998.

Carini, R., Kuh, G., and Klein, S. "Student Engagement and Student Learning: Testing the Linkages." *Research in Higher Education,* 2006, 33, 571–593.

Cross, P. *Beyond the Open Door: New Students in Higher Education.* San Francisco: Jossey-Bass, 1971.

Engstrom, C., and Tinto, V. *Pathways to Student Success: The Impact of Learning Communities on the Success of Academically Under-Prepared College Students. Final Report.* Palo Alto, Calif.: William and Flora Hewlett Foundation, 2006.

Gabelnick, F., MacGregor, J., Matthews, R., and Smith, B. (eds.). *Learning Communities: Creating Connections Among Students, Faculty, and Disciplines.* New Directions for Teaching and Learning, no. 41. San Francisco: Jossey-Bass, 1990.

Grubb, N., and Associates. (eds.). *Honored but Invisible: An Inside Look at Teaching in Community College.* London: Routledge, 1999.

Lamkin, M. "To Achieve the Dream, First Look at the Facts." *Change,* 2004, 36(6), 12–15.

Lindholm, J, Szelenyi, K., Hurtado, S., and Korn, W. *The American College Teacher: National Norms for the 2004–2005 HERI Faculty Survey.* Los Angeles: Higher Education Research Institute, University of California, Los Angeles, 2005.

Malnarich, G., and others. *The Pedagogy of Possibilities: Developmental Education, College-Level Studies, and Learning Communities.* Olympia, Wash.: Evergreen State College, 2003.

McClenney, K., and Greene, T. "A Tale of Two Students: Building a Culture of Engagement in the Community College." *About Campus,* 2005, 10(3), 2–7.

National Center for Education Statistics. *Remedial Education in Institutions of Higher Education in Fall 1995.* Washington, D.C.: U.S. Department of Education, 1997.

National Center for Education Statistics. *Descriptive Summary of 1995–96 Beginning Postsecondary Students: Six Years Later.* Washington D.C.: U.S. Office of Education, 2003.

National Center for Education Statistics. *The Condition of Education 2005.* Washington D.C.: U.S. Department of Education, Office of Educational Research and Improvement, 2005.

Nelson, A. "A New College with a New Idea." 1925–1928. In *Education and Democracy: The Meaning of Alexander Meiklejohn, 1872–1964.* Madison: University of Wisconsin Press, 2001.

Pascarella, E., and Terenzini, P. *How College Affects Students.* San Francisco: Jossey-Bass, 2005.

Smith, B., MacGregor, J., Matthews, R., and Gabelnick, F. *Learning Communities: Reforming Undergraduate Education.* San Francisco: Jossey-Bass, 2004.

Strauss, A., and Corbin, J. *Basics of Qualitative Research: Grounded Theory Procedures and Techniques.* Thousand Oaks, Calif.: Sage, 1990.

Tinto, V. *Leaving College: Rethinking the Causes and Cures of Student Attrition.* (2nd ed.) Chicago: University of Chicago Press, 1993.

Tinto, V. "Classrooms as Communities: Exploring the Educational Character of Student Persistence." *Journal of Higher Education,* 1997, *68,* 599–623.

Zhao, C., and Kuh, G. "Adding Value: Learning Communities and Student Engagement." *Research in Higher Education,* 2004, *45,* 115–136.

CATHY MCHUGH ENGSTROM is department chair of higher education at Syracuse University.

NEW DIRECTIONS FOR TEACHING AND LEARNING • DOI: 10.1002/tl

2

This chapter explores the relationships between indicators of student success such as persistence and student engagement in effective educational practices focusing on historically underrepresented populations.

Promoting Persistence and Success of Underrepresented Students: Lessons for Teaching and Learning

Jillian Kinzie, Robert Gonyea, Rick Shoup, George D. Kuh

Significant progress has been made over the past four decades in enrolling more students from historically underrepresented groups in U.S. colleges and universities. While total enrollment increased by about 40 percent overall, minority student enrollment increased by 146 percent, with Hispanic undergraduate enrollment greatly outpacing other racial/ethnic groups (Li, 2007). In addition, more students from all types of backgrounds, about a third being first-generation college goers, and students with a wider range of talents and abilities are coming to college.

Although these higher participation rates are encouraging, about half of high school graduates are unprepared to succeed academically in college (ACT, 2004a). Large numbers of students do not complete the academically challenging course work in high school necessary to do well in college, which contributes to low retention and graduation rates. According to the National Center for Educational Statistics (NCES), about 29 percent of all first-year students at four-year colleges and universities and about 41 percent of entering students at community colleges required remedial education (Parsad and Lewis, 2003). Furthermore, the six-year graduation rate for African American students and Latinos at baccalaureate institutions is only about 46 percent, far below the 60 percent rate for white students (Berkner, He, and Cataldi, 2002; Carey, 2004).

NEW DIRECTIONS FOR TEACHING AND LEARNING, no. 115, Fall 2008 © Wiley Periodicals, Inc.
Published online in Wiley InterScience (www.interscience.wiley.com) • DOI: 10.1002/tl.323

21

Low retention and college completion rates for all students and the racial/ethnic gap in graduation rates mean that too many students do not acquire the desired knowledge, skills, and competencies they need for the twenty-first century. Projected growth in minority student participation in postsecondary education (Hussar and Bailey, 2006), combined with the relatively low overall graduation rates of these students and external pressures for institutional accountability for student learning (Bok, 2006; Commission on the Future of Higher Education, 2006), have intensified the need to better understand the factors that influence student success in college and to be more intentional about creating effective teaching and learning environments.

In this chapter, we explore the relationships between indicators of student success such as persistence and student engagement in effective educational practices as measured by the National Survey of Student Engagement (NSSE), and such other factors as remedial course taking and course withdrawal rates, review the research, and propose data-based ways to address these issues.

Overview: Historically Underrepresented Student Retention

Students leave college for a variety of individual and institutional reasons (Bean, 1990; Cabrera, Casteneda, Nora, and Hengstler, 1992; Peltier, Laden, and Matranga, 1999; Tinto, 1993). Among the most common factors are student background characteristics; precollege academic experiences; structural characteristics of institutions such as mission, size, and selectivity; and interactions with faculty, staff, and peers. Some studies also show that race is a significant predictor of persistence (Astin, 1997; Murtaugh, Burns, and Schuster, 1999; Peltier, Laden, and Matranga, 1999).

Because the undergraduate experience of historically underrepresented students may differ from that of the white majority, the factors linked to student retention must be examined for different groups of students (Allen, 1999; Gaither, 2005; Gonzalez, 2000–2001; Gloria, Robinson Kurpius, Hamilton, and Wilson, 1999; Person and Christensen, 1996). Allen (1999) found that different variables predicted persistence of students of color compared with white students. For example, a student's high school rank, first-year college grade point average (GPA), and a self-reported measure of desire to complete college explained more of the variance in the retention of minority students from the first to second year of college, while high school rank, first-year college GPA, and parental education accounted for the retention of nonminority students. Some research indicates that in contrast to their white peers, students of color perceive the college environment to be less supportive and are thus less likely to persist to graduation (Carey, 2004; Pascarella and others, 1996).

Other factors linked with the persistence of underrepresented students are racially conscious retention constructs, including a "sense of belonging"

(Hurtado and Carter, 1996), "validation" (Nora, Barlow, and Crisp, 2005; Rendón, 1994), and stereotype threat (Murphy, Steele, and Gross, 2007; Steele, 1997). Given that student background characteristics and precollege academic experiences cannot be directly altered by college or university faculty or staff, we must better understand the factors that can be influenced. Indeed, as Bensimon (2007) suggested, faculty and staff behavior are key variables in helping underrepresented students succeed in college.

Student Engagement and Retention

One line of inquiry that promises to increase our understanding and ability to improve student success in college is the research showing the positive links between student engagement in educationally purposeful activities and such desired outcomes as good grades, educational gains, and higher first-to-second year persistence and graduation rates (Astin, 1993; Kuh and others, 2005; Pascarella and Terenzini, 1991, 2005). Student engagement represents two critical features: the extent to which students take part in educationally effective practices and the degree to which the institution organizes productive activities for student learning. Among engaging educational practices are those summarized by Chickering and Gamson (1987): student-faculty contact, cooperation among students, active learning, prompt feedback, time on task, high expectations, and respect for diverse talents and ways of learning. Notably, most of these practices are within the purview of the classroom and represent activities that can be shaped to varying degrees through teaching practices and by creating environmental conditions that foster engagement.

The NSSE annually obtains information from four-year colleges and universities nationwide about student participation in empirically confirmed good practices in undergraduate education. Although NSSE was not designed as a tool to study retention at the institutional level, colleges and universities have used their results to gain insight into student persistence and suggest institutional action (Kuh, 2001, 2003). For example, at the institutional level of analysis, strong positive correlations exist between graduation rates and scores on the five NSSE clusters of effective educational practice: academic challenge, active and collaborative learning, student-faculty interaction, enriching educational experiences, and supportive campus environment (Kuh and others, 2007).

Engagement and Underrepresented Students in Higher Education. Students from all racial/ethnic backgrounds benefit from participating in educationally effective activities. However, some researchers have found that historically underrepresented students are not able to take full advantage of learning opportunities, especially at predominantly white institutions (PWIs) (Feagin, Vera, and Imani, 1996; Swail, Cabrera, Lee, and Williams, 2005; Turner, 1994). The limiting factors are attributed to substandard precollege educational preparation, students' family socioeconomic and educational backgrounds, racial discrimination and—for Latino students in particular—tensions between familial obligations, and educational aspirations (Bridges, Kinzie, Nelson Laird, and Kuh, 2008; Dayton, Gonzalez-Vasquez, Martinez, and Plum, 2004; Ortiz, 2004).

Increasing evidence suggests that a small number of programs and activities engage students at high levels and increase educational gains and student persistence. These activities include first-year seminars, learning communities, service-learning, undergraduate research, study abroad and other experiences with diversity, internships, and capstone courses and projects. The Association of American Colleges and Universities identified these promising high-impact practices in its 2007 report, *College Learning for the New Global Century*. Although these practices are growing in popularity, NSSE results and other national data indicate that participation in these activities varies among historically underrepresented students. For example, first-generation students and transfer students were less likely than other students to participate in a learning community, a research project with a faculty member, study abroad, or a culminating senior experience (National Survey of Student Engagement, 2007). African American, Latino, and Asian American/Pacific Islanders participated in senior culminating experiences (senior project, internship, practicum, co-op) at lower levels, and fewer African American and Asian Pacific Islanders studied abroad than did white students. The racial/ethnic participation gaps in high-impact practices illustrate lingering inequities in the undergraduate experience.

Academic Policies and Practice: Remedial Course Taking and Course Withdrawals. Remedial course work in postsecondary education has proliferated to respond to what ACT (2004b) declared as the "college readiness crisis." According to Bettinger and Long (2005), about one-third of entering college students take developmental courses to bring their academic skills up to a level that will allow them to perform adequately in college. More than a quarter of four-year college students who have to take three or more remedial classes leave college after the first year (National Research Council, 2004). However, relatively little is known about the role of completion rates for individual courses and student persistence (Adelman, 1995; Dunwoody and Frank, 1995).

According to Adelman (1995, 2006), students who accumulated excessive withdrawals, incompletes, and no-credit repeats greatly increased their time to degree and cut in half their chances of earning a degree. As time-to-degree increases, so does the overall cost of college. Combined, these factors reduce the likelihood of persistence. Academic policies such as remediation and course withdrawal represent aspects of the educational program that faculty members control and can monitor and influence in their departments and at the course level. Yet we have a limited understanding of the extent to which these practices have a differential impact on underrepresented students.

NEW DIRECTIONS FOR TEACHING AND LEARNING • DOI: 10.1002/tl

Analyzing the Relationship Between Student Engagement and Success

Considerable scholarly research has been directed at understanding student success. The Connecting the Dots (CTD) project (Kuh and others, 2006) analyzed the relationship between educational practices and the success of students historically underrepresented in higher education. In that study, we examined academic transcript data—such as first-year GPA, persistence to the second year of study, and senior grades, combined with NSSE results from 6,200 first-year students and 5,227 seniors at eighteen diverse colleges and universities, which included four historically black colleges and universities (HBCUs) and three HSIs (Hispanic-serving institutions). Briefly, the methods of analysis employed in the CTD study included ordinary least squares and logistic regression to estimate models for the general effects of engagement in educationally purposeful activities (see the list in the chapter appendix) on GPA and persistence to the second year of college and tests for the presence of conditional or interaction effects. Table 2.1 shows the net effects of engagement on the success indicators from the CTD study after controlling for student background characteristics, precollege ability, college enrollment characteristics, and other time on task behaviors.

Engagement and Persistence to the Second Year. Returning for a second year of college is an important measure because it has a significant impact on graduation rates (Gardner, Upcraft, and Barefoot, 2005). Four findings from the CTD study are instructive for teaching and learning.

Table 2.1. Effects of Engagement on Success Indicators from the Connecting the Dots Project

	Persistence to the Second Year	First-Year GPA	Senior GPA
	Unstandardized B	Unstandardized B	Unstandardized B
Engagement measures			
Six to twenty hours per week studying[a]	−.02	.04*	.02
Twenty-one or more hours per week studying[a]	−.12	.12***	.08***
Educationally purposeful activities (standardized)[b]	.15***	.04***	.07***

Note: Model covariates included gender, race, first-generation status, parental income, graduate degree expectations, high school honors course work, high school cocurricular activities, high school GPA, precollege achievement score, merit grants, credit hours earned, commuter status, transfer status, and time spent working, relaxing/socializing, and cocurricular activities. The persistence model also included first-year GPA and unmet financial need. The persistence model used logistic regression, and GPA models used ordinary least squares regression. B values are unstandardized coefficients.

[a]Compared with students who studied five hours or fewer per week.

[b]See the appendix at the end of the chapter.

New Directions for Teaching and Learning • DOI: 10.1002/tl

First, student engagement had a positive, statistically significant effect on persistence, even after controlling for background characteristics, other college experiences during the first college year, academic achievement, and financial aid. To put this in perspective, students who are engaged at a level that is one standard deviation below the average have a probability of returning of .85, whereas students who are engaged at a level that is one standard deviation above the average have a probability of returning of .91.

Second, whether students spent their time on academic tasks such as studying or on nonacademic tasks such as relaxing and socializing or working off-campus did not affect the probability of their returning to the same institution for the second year. This finding is not surprising given the offsetting effects of these experiences (positive for studying, negative for working off campus) on first-year GPA, which was also included in the model. Being involved in cocurricular activities, however, had a strong positive impact on students' probability of returning for the second year of college (Kuh and others, 2006). The link between extracurricular involvements and persistence is well documented empirically (Astin, 1993; Pascarella and Terenzini, 1983, 2005) and theoretically (Astin, 1984; Tinto, 1993).

Third, students with high school grades of mostly Bs had a higher probability of returning for the second year of college than students who earned either mostly A grades or C grades. Similarly, students with average high school achievement scores had the greatest odds of returning, while students with the lowest and highest achievement scores were less likely to return. These findings regarding achievement levels and persistence tend to be related to student satisfaction and if the student is attending the first-choice institution. Fourth, the effects of engagement on persistence to the second year vary for students from different racial or ethnic backgrounds. In terms of persistence, African American students benefit more than white students do from increasing their engagement in educationally effective activities. Although African American students at the lowest levels of engagement are less likely to persist than their white counterparts, African Americans become more likely than white students to return for a second year as their engagement increases. There are no differences for other racial and ethnic groups in terms of the effects of engagement on persistence. This finding is important since it indicates that engagement has a compensatory effect on persistence to the second year of college at the same institution for African American students.

Academic Policies and Practice: Remedial Course Taking and Course Withdrawals. For the purposes of this chapter, we conducted additional descriptive analyses on the CTD data to study the relationship of remedial, or basic skills, course work (courses addressing subjects such as numeracy and computational skills, literacy and communication skills, general skills, and second-language skills) and course withdrawals to engagement and persistence. We were limited by the fact that only five of the eighteen institutions had a substantial number (at least 20 percent) of students who took basic skills courses. Thus, the analysis used a subset of the

CTD data: 1,336 full-time first-year students. Students were grouped into three categories: (1) those who attempted no basic skills course hours (n = 790); (2) those who attempted up to three basic skills course hours, presumably one course (n = 398); and (3) those who attempted more than three basic skills course hours, presumably more than one course (n = 148). Three scales were used for this analysis:

- *Engagement in active learning.* A scale compiling twenty-five academic and classroom-focused engagement items, including various interactions with faculty; course work emphasizing higher-order mental activities; spending time in academic preparation; participating in class discussions, group work, and presentations; and writing papers.
- *Perception of social and academic support.* Seven items captured students' perceptions of the campus environment in terms of support for academics, nonacademic responsibilities, and social development; emphasis on diverse experiences; and relationships among students, administrative personnel, and faculty.
- *Self-reported academic gains.* Eight items collected students' self-reported progress in general education learning, specifically in writing, speaking, thinking critically, analyzing quantitative problems, using information technology, learning effectively on their own, and general education. The students' ratings of the extent to which the institution emphasizes spending significant amounts of time studying and on academic work are also included.

The effects of remedial course taking on student persistence and success are complex and mixed. Table 2.2 shows that persistence rates were 16 percent lower for students who attempted more than three hours of basic courses, ranging from 91 percent among students in the first two groups to 75 percent for the third group. Moreover, precollege test scores did not explain this pattern. That is, when only students with lower ACT scores (or SAT equivalent) were included, the persistence rate was still 15 percent lower for students taking more than three hours of basic skills course work.

Although the persistence rate drops for students who complete more remedial courses, students who took more than three basic skills course hours were more engaged in active learning than their peers on average (Table 2.2). It may be that remedial course curricula require these students to put more effort into their studies and devote more time on task to learning basic academic skills. It may also be that students taking remedial courses were less likely to enroll in large lecture courses, math and science courses, and other classroom settings that less frequently employ active and collaborative learning approaches. The same pattern emerged for student perceptions of the social and academic environment and their self-reported gains. This is understandable since students who start college with academic deficiencies may perceive more support from the institution and also believe they have made

Table 2.2. Mean Comparisons by Attempted Basic Skills Course Hours, Overall and for Subpopulations by Race and First-Generation Status

	Number of Students	Number of Attempted Basic Skills Course Hours			Significance[a]
		None (n = 790)	Up to Three (n = 398)	More than Three (n = 148)	
Persistence to the second year					
Overall	1,336	.91	.91	.75	***
African American	221	.88	.91	.74	+
Latino	280	.89	.89	.77	*
White	725	.91	.91	.70	**
First generation	593	.89	.87	.70	***
First-year GPA					
Overall	1,336	2.94	2.89	2.51	***
African American	221	2.71	2.52	2.29	***
Latino	280	2.84	2.76	2.61	**
White	725	3.01	3.04	2.41	***
First generation	593	2.86	2.74	2.41	***
Active learning					
Overall	1,336	50.1	48.9	52.2	***
African American	221	51.2	51.5	53.2	
Latino	280	52.4	49.0	52.1	+
White	725	49.4	48.6	50.2	
First generation	593	50.3	49.6	51.1	
Institutional support for academic success					
Overall	1,336	49.7	50.0	51.8	+
African American	221	48.5	49.2	52.4	
Latino	280	51.1	49.1	52.6	
White	725	49.7	50.9	48.3	
First generation	593	50.0	50.1	52.7	
General academic gains (self-reported)					
Overall	1,336	49.7	49.8	52.2	+
African American	221	50.9	50.8	52.7	**
Latino	280	53.0	51.4	53.5	
White	725	48.4	49.0	46.5	
First generation	593	50.4	50.7	52.6	

Note: One-way ANOVA results for mean comparisons.

[a]Significance levels of F-tests for between-group differences: $^+p < .10$. $^*p < .05$. $^{**}p < .01$. $^{***}p < .001$.

NEW DIRECTIONS FOR TEACHING AND LEARNING • DOI: 10.1002/tl

considerable academic progress given their basic academic skills and competencies prior to college.

Finally, black and Latino students took substantially more basic skills course hours than white students did. Although the results indicated that white students in general are less engaged in active learning activities and report less academic progress in their learning, black students tend to perceive their campus academic and social environments to be less supportive. At the same time, these relationships were generally consistent regardless of how many basic skills course hours were attempted. First-generation students were somewhat more likely than their peers with college-educated parents to take remedial course work. However, first-generation students who took more basic skills course hours were less likely to persist and were less engaged than their peers with college-educated parents who took the same number of remedial course hours.

According to Adelman (1999, 2006), course completion patterns (drops, withdrawals, incomplete grades, or repeats) are a drag on bachelor degree completion rates of students at four-year colleges. The first-year student CTD data reveal that 63 percent of students completed all of their attempted hours (Table 2.3). The remaining students were distributed fairly evenly among three categories: (1) those who did not complete 1 to 10 percent of attempted hours, (2) those who did not complete 11 to 20 percent of attempted hours, and (3) those who did not complete more than 20 percent of attempted hours. In general, these data indicate that taking more than three basic skills course hours is associated with a higher percentage of unearned course hours. Yet taking some but not more than three basic

Table 2.3. Cross-Tabulation of Course Hours Completion Categories by Attempted Basic Skills Course Hours

		Attempted Basic Skills Course Hours (%)			
	Number of Students	None (n = 790)	Up to Three (n = 398)	More than Three (n = 148)	Total
					1,336
Completed all hours attempted	846	66.2%	67.3%	37.2%	63.3%
Did not complete 1 to 10 percent	133	11.4	6.8	10.8	10.0
Did not complete 11 to 20 percent	185	11.4	14.3	25.7	13.8
Did not complete more than 20 percent	172	11.0	11.6	26.4	12.9
Total	1,336	100.0	100.0	100.0	100.0

skills course hours seems to be unrelated to unearned course hours. Also, as expected, scores on all the dependent measures steadily declined as students completed fewer attempted hours. Black and Latino students were more likely to have unearned credits than white students, which is consistent with the lower six-year graduation rates for blacks and Latinos (Berkner He, and Cataldi, 2002; Carey, 2004).

Addressing the Retention Challenge in Teaching and Learning

In this section we discuss eight recommendations and their implications for teaching and learning based on the findings reported here.

First, new students tend to benefit from early interventions and sustained attention during the first year in terms of their academic performance. The CTD findings suggest that institutions would be wise to focus early efforts on students from historically underrepresented backgrounds and those with low ACT scores. To do this effectively, a school must first understand who its students are, what they are prepared to do academically, and what they expect of the institution and themselves. For example, given the benefits that time on task and engagement confer in terms of college grades, it is wise to send clear messages to students through precollege mentoring programs and sustained interactions with faculty and staff throughout the first year about the value of engagement and what students who succeed do on this particular campus. For example, all educators—faculty, student life professionals, academic advisers, and so on—need to coach students in the development of expected study habits. Experiences early in the first year set in place patterns of behavior that will endure over students' years in college (Howard, 2005; Schilling and Schilling, 2005). This requires that students are introduced to the approach to studying in the particular course or discipline, that campus space (campus living units, libraries, student unions) is conducive to studying, and that advisers counsel students on ways to make cocurricular involvements supportive of academic success. Faculty members, advisers, and student affairs professionals must clearly and consistently communicate to students what is expected of them and provide periodic feedback as to the quality of students' performance.

Second, faculty teaching first-year courses have the greatest opportunity to shape student behaviors in terms of time on task and engagement. This is important because students learn more when they are intensely involved in their education and are asked to think about and apply what they are learning. Student time on task can be increased by using such active and collaborative learning activities as classroom-based problem solving, peer teaching, service-learning, and various forms of electronic technologies that induce students to work with peers on projects during and outside class, as well as assign writing tasks that require multiple drafts.

Active and collaborative learning approaches are educationally effective when they are aligned with a wider range of student learning styles and feature three fundamentals to fostering student learning: involving students, increasing their time on task, and taking advantage of peer influence. To illustrate, faculty can assign short problem-based activities that require students to work in teams in and out of the classroom; this practice increases students' investment in preparing for class by requiring them to submit an online assignment dependent on assigned readings, and it illustrates the value of drafting and peer review by having students read one another's papers before they turn them in to help them locate errors before being graded. This does not mean lecturing is no longer an appropriate instructional approach, but rather that more faculty should employ a greater repertoire of teaching methods to engage diverse learning styles.

Humboldt State University used its NSSE results to gain insights into the engagement patterns of students who persisted compared to those who withdrew. Results indicated that students who withdrew were less likely to work with their classmates on class assignments than students who persisted (Hughes and Pace, 2003). These results prompted faculty members to structure more collaborative learning in first-year courses and facilitate the formation of study groups and the institution to consider implementing learning communities to increase opportunities for students to interact with their classmates.

Third, fundamental to effective teaching is the belief that every student can learn under the right conditions. This "talent development" philosophy requires that faculty embrace and address students' diverse talents and needs (Astin, 1985; Chickering, 2006; Chickering and Gamson, 1987). Although a talent development philosophy is appropriate for all students, it is particularly effective for working with students historically underserved in higher education, especially when pedagogical practices acknowledge and honor the experiences of learners and view the talents and skills students bring to the classroom as assets rather than deficiencies. Turner's suggestion (1999) for rethinking pedagogical practice is instructive: resist the stance that students' lack of preparation for class is caused by defects in student character or other cultural distractions and instead take the position that students come to college able to do the work but with no clear sense of what they should be doing and why this is important for learning and success. This position requires faculty members to accept that in times of increasingly diverse student populations, it is necessary to make clear the demands of academic work and spell out what students need to do. Such a view holds that because each student has a unique perspective on the world and the topic under study, all students enrich the learning of others as well as their own through sharing their knowledge and experience (Alexander and Murphy, 1994).

Uri Treisman (1992) developed pioneering teaching strategies for working with students from historically underserved groups at the University of

California, Berkeley, who were failing calculus even though they had the academic prerequisites and demonstrated ability to perform successfully. Treisman's strategies were grounded in a talent development perspective: "We did not question that minority students could excel. We just wanted to know what kind of setting we would need to provide so that they could" (p. 368). Given that engaging practices, such as active and collaborative learning, paid off more in terms of first-year GPA for students with lower entering achievement scores, faculty should use a variety of teaching approaches to reach a range of student abilities. For example, first-generation students who report more participation in group discussion, presentations, and group projects and who more frequently discuss courses with other students have been found to have a higher probability of academic success and retention (Amelink, 2005). Preferred learning styles may explain some of the difference in that "lower-ability" students tend to perform better when course material is presented in concrete terms and they have opportunities to apply concepts to their daily lives.

Fourth, institutions must create interconnected learning support networks, including early warning systems and safety nets, and tie students and faculty who are teaching first-year and remedial courses to them in intentional ways. Students attending institutions that employ a comprehensive system of complementary initiatives based on effective educational practices are more likely to perform better academically, be more satisfied, and persist. These include well-designed and well-implemented placement testing; first-year seminars; learning communities; early warning systems; redundant safety nets; supplemental instruction; peer tutoring and mentoring; theme-based campus housing; adequate financial aid, including on-campus work; internships; service-learning; and demonstrably effective teaching practices (Kuh and others, 2005; Wang and Grimes, 2001). However, simply offering such programs and practices does not guarantee that they will have the intended effects on student success. In fact, far fewer students use campus learning and support services than say they will when starting college (NSSE, 2005). Institutional programs and practices must not only be of high quality and customized to meet the needs of students they are intended to reach (Kuh and others, 2005); they must also be intentionally connected to students, courses, and faculty to increase the likelihood that students will take full advantage of the programs; in effect, they must be unavoidable.

Fifth, given the educational value of participating in high-impact activities and data showing that historically underrepresented students participate in these experiences at a lower level than their peers, it is important to structure curricular requirements that make it possible for every student to do one or more of these activities. If a student perceives that the cost of staying in school or becoming involved in a certain activity—such as an internship, undergraduate research, or study abroad—outweighs the return on investment, he or she may forgo the opportunity and leave college prematurely (Braxton, 2003). Similarly, if a student does not expect to do research with a faculty member or take part in study abroad, chances are that opportunities to pursue these activities will be overlooked or dismissed out of hand.

Sixth, faculty and staff also must employ practices that make a difference to underrepresented student retention. Rendón (1994) found that validation—an enabling, confirming, and supportive process initiated by faculty and other agents of socialization in and out of the classroom—fosters student success, particularly for historically underserved students. Validation activities in the teaching and learning context include calling students by name, working one-on-one with students, praising students, providing encouragement and support, encouraging students to see themselves as capable of learning, and providing vehicles for students to support and praise each other. These validation actions can induce transformational changes in students, accompanied by an increased interest and confidence in their capacity to learn. Helping faculty members acquire approaches to validate students should be a priority for faculty development programs.

Seventh, because students taking a heavier remedial course load are more likely to leave college, and with students of color and first-generation students represented in greater numbers among those taking remedial courses, institutions that are able to tailor remediation programs to the specific social, cultural, and educational characteristics of students in need of such assistance may become more adept at moving students from developmental courses to success in college-level courses and, most important, persistence to graduation. Moreover, given that black and Latino students were more likely to have unearned credits than white students and that scores on all the engagement measures declined as students completed fewer attempted hours, it is crucial to ensure that historically underrepresented students understand academic policies and the implications of withdrawing from courses. At the same time, faculty members should learn more about the experiences of students in remedial courses, the status of course withdrawal policy and practice in their department, and the effect on students of color, and learn to identify curricular trouble spots—courses in which students earn high rates of Ds and Fs, withdrawals, and incompletes—to develop more effective approaches to address challenges to student success.

Finally, the talent development view must also be operationalized at an institutional level. This requires that the campus organize its resources and create conditions for teaching and learning based on educationally effective practices. When these conditions complement the institution's mission and values, they create powerful learning environments that lead to desirable learning outcomes for all students. Moreover, faculty and staff can address shortcomings in students' academic preparation and increase the chances that students will succeed by adapting demonstrably effective policies and practices. Most important, some students may not know how to become engaged, or they may not feel entitled to being engaged, particularly if it involves requests for help, or they may avoid the activities that signify engagement to avoid failure or the risk of rejection. In predominantly white campuses, minority students may consciously decide not to speak out in class or initiate a conversation with a faculty member outside class for fear of being stereotyped (Bensimon, 2007; Peña, Bensimon, and Colyar, 2006; Steele, 1997).

Conclusion

Students would be well served by colleges and universities that use educationally effective practices throughout the institution. At the same time, emphasizing the engagement of students at the lower ranges of ACT scores could well increase their chances of earning good college grades in the critical first year. In particular, what faculty do in terms of structuring engaging opportunities into their courses, coupled with a healthy measure of prompt feedback, are essential to shaping such desirable student academic performance (Kuh, Nelson Laird, and Umbach, 2004). Even more, efforts to create more hospitable campus environments for underrepresented students must be culturally sensitive and strive to employ engaging educational practices that make a difference to student success.

Appendix: Educationally Purposeful Activities

Following is the summative scale of nineteen NSSE items measuring student interaction with faculty, their experiences with diverse others, and their involvement in opportunities for active and collaborative learning:

- Asked questions in class or contributed to class discussions
- Made a class presentation
- Prepared two or more drafts of a paper or assignment before turning it in
- Come to class without completing readings or assignments
- Worked with other students on projects during class
- Worked with classmates outside of class to prepare class assignments
- Tutored or taught other students (paid or voluntary)
- Participated in a community-based project as part of a regular course
- Used an electronic medium (list-serv, chat group, Internet, etc.) to discuss or complete an assignment
- Used e-mail to communicate with an instructor
- Discussed grades or assignments with an instructor
- Talked about career plans with a faculty member or advisor
- Discussed ideas from your readings or classes with faculty members outside of class
- Received prompt feedback from faculty on your academic performance (written or oral)
- Worked harder than you thought you could to meet an instructor's standards or expectations

NEW DIRECTIONS FOR TEACHING AND LEARNING • DOI: 10.1002/tl

- Worked with faculty members on activities other than coursework (committees, orientation, student life activities, etc.)
- Discussed ideas from your readings or classes with others outside of class (students, family members, coworkers, etc.)
- Had serious conversations with students of a different race or ethnicity than your own
- Had serious conversations with students who differ from you in terms of their religious beliefs, political opinions, or personal values

Cronbach's alpha coefficient for internal consistency for first-year students was .818, and for seniors it was .836. The NSSE response set for 2000 was Very Often, Often, Occasionally, and Never. For 2001–2003, it was Very Often, Often, Sometimes, and Never.

References

ACT. *ACT National Data Release.* Iowa City, Ia.: ACT, 2004a.

ACT. *Crisis at the Core: Preparing All Students for College and Work.* Iowa City, Ia.: ACT, 2004b.

Adelman, C. *The New College Course Map and Transcript Files: Changes in Course-Taking and Achievement, 1972–1993.* Washington, D.C.: U.S. Department of Education, Office of Educational Research and Improvement, 1995.

Adelman, C. *Answers in the Toolbox: Academic Intensity, Attendance Patterns, and Bachelor's Degree Attainment.* Washington, D.C.: U.S. Department of Education, Office of Educational Research and Improvement, 1999.

Adelman, C. *The Toolbox Revisited: Paths to Degree Completion from High School Through College.* Washington, D.C.: U.S. Department of Education, Office of Vocational and Adult Education, 2006.

Alexander, P. A., and Murphy, P. K. "The Research Base for APA's Learner-Centered Psychological Principles." Paper presented at the annual meeting of the American Educational Research Association, New Orleans, La., Apr. 1994.

Allen, W. R. "The Color of Success: African-American College Student Outcomes at Predominately White and Historically Black Public Colleges and Universities." *Harvard Educational Review,* 1999, *62*(1), 26–44.

Amelink, C. T. "Predicting Academic Success Among First-Year, First Generation Students." Unpublished doctoral dissertation, Virginia Polytechnic Institute and State University, 2005.

Association of American Colleges and Universities. *College Learning for the New Global Century.* Washington, D.C.: Association of American Colleges and Universities, 2007.

Astin, A. W. "Student Involvement: A Developmental Theory for Higher Education." *Journal of College Student Development,* 1984, *25*(4), 297–308.

Astin, A. W. "Involvement: The Cornerstone of Excellence." *Change,* 1985, *17*(4), 35–39.

Astin, A. W. *What Matters in College? Four Critical Years Revisited.* San Francisco: Jossey-Bass, 1993.

Astin, A. W. "How 'Good' Is Your Institution's Retention Rate?" *Research in Higher Education,* 1997, *38*(6), 647–658.

Bean, J. P. "Why Students Leave: Insights from Research." In D. Hossler and J. P. Bean (eds.), *The Strategic Management of College Enrollments.* San Francisco: Jossey-Bass, 1990.

Bensimon, E. M. "The Underestimated Significance of Practitioner Knowledge in the Scholarship on Student Success." *Review of Higher Education,* 2007, *30*(4), 441–469.

Berkner, L., He, S., and Cataldi, E. F. *Descriptive Summary of 1995–96 Beginning Postsecondary Students. Six Years Later.* Washington, D.C.: U.S. Department of Education, National Center for Education Statistics, 2002.

Bettinger, E. P., and Long, B. T. "Addressing the Needs of Under-Prepared Students in Higher Education: Does College Remediation Work?" Cambridge, Mass.: National Bureau of Economic Research, May 2005.

Bok, D. *Our Underachieving Colleges.* Princeton, N.J.: Princeton University Press, 2006.

Braxton, J. M. "Student Success." In S. R. Komives and D. B. Woodard Jr. (eds.), *Student Services: A Handbook for the Profession.* (4th ed.) San Francisco: Jossey-Bass, 2003.

Bridges, B. K., Kinzie, J., Nelson Laird, T. F., and Kuh, G. D. "Student Engagement and Success at Minority Serving Institutions." In M. Gasman, B. Baez, and C.S.V. Turner (eds.), *Understanding Minority-Serving Institutions.* Albany, N.Y.: SUNY Press, 2008.

Cabrera, A. F., Casteneda, M. B., Nora, A., and Hengstler, D. "The Convergence Between Two Theories of College Persistence." *Journal of Higher Education,* 1992, *63*(2), 143–164.

Carey, K. *A Matter of Degrees: Improving Graduation Rates in Four-Year Colleges and Universities.* Washington, D.C.: Education Trust, 2004.

Chickering, A. W. "Every Student Can Learn If . . . . " *About Campus,* 2006, *2*(2), 9–15.

Chickering, A. W., and Gamson, Z. F. (eds.). "Seven Principles for Good Practice in Undergraduate Education." *AAHE Bulletin,* 1987, *39,* 3–7.

Commission on the Future of Higher Education. *A Test of Leadership: Charting the Future of U.S. Higher Education.* Washington, D.C.: U.S. Department of Education, 2006.

Dayton, B., Gonzalez-Vasquez, N., Martinez, C. R., and Plum, C. "Hispanic-Serving Institutions Through the Eyes of Students and Administrators." In A. M. Ortiz (ed.), *Addressing the Unique Needs of Latino American Students.* New Directions for Student Services, no. 105. San Francisco: Jossey-Bass, 2004.

Dunwoody, P. T., and Frank, M. L. "Why Students Withdraw from Classes." *Journal of Psychology,* 1995, *129*(5), 553–559.

Feagin, J. R., Vera, H., and Imani, N. *The Agony of Education: Black Students at White Colleges and Universities.* New York: Routledge, 1996.

Gaither, G. H. "Editor's Notes." In G. H. Gaither (ed.), *Minority Retention: What Works?* New Directions for Institutional Research, no. 125. San Francisco: Jossey-Bass, 2005.

Gardner, J. N., Upcraft, M. L., and Barefoot, B. "Principles of Good Practice for the First College Year and Summary of Recommendations." In M. Upcraft and Associates (eds.), *Challenging and Supporting The First-Year Student.* San Francisco: Jossey-Bass, 2005.

Gloria, A. M., Robinson Kurpius, S. E., Hamilton, K. D., and Wilson, M. S. "African American Students' Persistence at a Predominantly White University: Influences of Social Support, University Comfort, and Self-Beliefs." *Journal of College Student Development,* 1999, *40,* 257–268.

Gonzalez, K. P. "Toward a Theory of Minority Student Participation in Predominantly White Colleges and Universities." *Journal of College Student Retention,* 2000–2001, *2*(1), 69–91.

Howard, J. A. "Why Should We Care About Student Expectations?" In T. E. Miller and Associates (eds.), *Promoting Reasonable Expectations: Aligning Student and Institutional Views of the College Experience.* San Francisco: Jossey-Bass, 2005.

Hughes, R., and Pace, C. R. "Using NSSE to Study Student Retention and Withdrawal." *Assessment Update,* 2003, *15*(4), 1–2, 15.

Hurtado, S., and Carter, D. F. (1996). "Latino Students' Sense of Belonging in the College Community: Rethinking the Concept of Integration on Campus." In F. K. Stage, G. L. Anaya, J. P. Bean, D. Hossler, and G. Kuh (eds.), *College Students: Evolving Nature of Research* (pp. 123–136). Needham Heights, Mass.: Simon & Schuster.

Hussar, W., and Bailey, T. M. *Projections of Education Statistics to 2015 (NCES 2006–084).* Washington, D.C.: U.S. Department of Education, National Center for Education Statistics, Institute of Education Sciences, 2006.

Kuh, G. D. "Assessing What Really Matters to Student Learning: Inside the National Survey of Student Engagement." *Change*, 2001, *33*(3), 10–17, 66.

Kuh, G. D. "What We're Learning About Student Engagement from NSSE: Benchmarks for Effective Educational Practices." *Change*, 2003, *35*(2), 24–32.

Kuh, G. D. "Student Engagement in the First Year of College." In M. L. Upcraft, J. N. Gardner, and B. O. Barefoot (eds.), *Challenging and Supporting the First-Year Student: A Handbook for Improving the First Year of College.* San Francisco: Jossey-Bass, 2005.

Kuh, G. D., Nelson Laird T. F., and Umbach, P. D. "Aligning Faculty and Student Behavior: Realizing the Promise of Greater Expectations." *Liberal Education*, 2004, *90*(4), 24–31.

Kuh, G. D., and others. *Student Success in College: Creating Conditions That Matter.* San Francisco: Jossey-Bass, 2005.

Kuh, G. D., and others. *Connecting the Dots: Multi-Faceted Analyses of the Relationships Between Student Engagement Results from the NSSE, and the Institutional Practices and Conditions That Foster Student Success: Final Report Prepared for Lumina Foundation for Education.* Bloomington: Indiana University, Center for Postsecondary Research, 2006.

Kuh, G. D., and others. *Piecing Together the Student Success Puzzle: Research, Propositions, and Recommendations.* ASHE Higher Education Report, vol. 32, no. 5. San Francisco: Jossey-Bass, 2007.

Li, X. *Characteristics of Minority-Serving Institutions and Minority Undergraduates Enrolled in These Institutions.* Washington, D.C.: U.S. Department of Education, National Center for Education Statistics, Institute of Education Sciences, 2007.

Murphy, M. C., Steele, C. M., and Gross, J. J. "Signaling Threat: How Situational Cues Affect Women in Math, Science, and Engineering Settings." *Psychological Science*, 2007, *18*(10), 879–885.

Murtaugh, P. A., Burns, L. D., and Schuster, J. "Predicting the Retention of University Students." *Research in Higher Education*, 1999, *40*(3), 355–371.

National Center for Education Statistics. "Data on Student Participation in Remedial Courses by Racial Ethnic Groups." 2008. Retrieved Jan. 8, 2008, from http://nces.ed.gov/.

National Research Council. *Engaging Schools: Fostering High School Students' Motivation to Learn.* Washington, D.C.: National Academies Press, 2004.

National Survey of Student Engagement. *Student Engagement: Experiences That Matter: Enhancing Student Learning and Success.* Bloomington: Indiana University Center for Postsecondary Research, 2007.

National Survey of Student Engagement. *Student Engagement: Exploring Different Dimensions of Student Engagement.* Bloomington: Indiana University Center for Postsecondary Research, 2005.

Nora, A., Barlow, E., and Crisp, G. "Student Persistence and Degree Attainment Beyond the First Year in College." In A. Seidman (ed.), *College Student Retention: Formula for Student Success.* Westport, Conn.: ACE/Praeger, 2005.

Ortiz, A. M. "Promoting the Success of Latino Students: A Call to Action." In A. M. Ortiz (ed.), *Addressing the Unique Needs of Latino American Students.* New Directions for Student Services, no. 105. San Francisco: Jossey-Bass, 2004.

Parsad, B., and Lewis, L. *Remedial Education at Degree-Granting Postsecondary Institutions in Fall 2000.* Washington, D.C.: U.S. Department of Education, National Center for Education Statistics, 2003.

Pascarella, E. T., and others. "Influences on Students' Openness to Diversity and Challenge in the First Year of College." *Journal of Higher Education*, 1996, *67*(2), 174–195.

Pascarella, E. T., and Terenzini, P. T. "Predicting Voluntary Freshman Year Persistence/Withdrawal Behavior in a Residential University: A Path Analytic Validation of Tinto's Model." *Journal of Educational Psychology*, 1983, *75*, 215–226.

Pascarella, E. T., and Terenzini, P. T. *How College Affects Students: A Third Decade of Research.* San Francisco: Jossey-Bass, 2005.

Pascarella, E. T., and Terenzini, P. T. *How College Affects Students: Findings and Insights from Twenty-Years of Research.* San Francisco: Jossey-Bass, 1991.

Peltier, G., Laden, R., and Matranga, M.. "Student Persistence in College." *Journal of College Student Retention,* 1999, *1*(4), 357–375.

Peña, E. V., Bensimon, E. M., and Colyar, J. "Contextual Problem Defining: Learning to Think and Act from the Standpoint of Equity." *Liberal Education,* 2006, *92*(2), 48–55.

Person, D., and Christensen, M. C. "Understanding Black Student Culture and Black Student Retention." *NASPA Journal,* 1996, *34,* 47–56.

Rendón, L. "Validating Culturally Diverse Students: Toward a New Model of Learning and Student Development." *Innovation in Higher Education,* 1994, *19,* 33–52

Schilling, K. M., and Schilling, K. L. "Expectations and Performance." In L. M. Upcraft, J. N. Gardner, and B. O. Barefoot (eds.), *Challenging and Supporting the First-Year Student: A Handbook for Improving the First Year of College.* San Francisco: Jossey-Bass, 2005.

Steele, C. M. "A Threat in the Air: How Stereotypes Shape Intellectual Identity and Performance." *American Psychologist,* 1997, *52,* 613–629.

Swail, W. S., Cabrera, A. F., Lee, C., and Williams, A. *Latino Students and the Educational Pipelines: A Three-Part Series. Part III: Pathways to the Bachelor's Degree for Latino Students.* Stafford, Va.: Education Policy Institute, 2005.

Tinto, V. *Leaving College: Rethinking the Causes and Cures of Student Attrition.* (2nd ed.) Chicago: University of Chicago Press, 1993.

Treisman, U. "Studying Students Studying Calculus: A Look at the Lives of Minority Mathematics Students in College." *College Mathematics Journal,* 1992, *23*(5), 362–372.

Turner, C.S.V. "Guests in Someone Else's House: Students of Color." *Review of Higher Education,* 1994, *17*(4), 355–370.

Turner, R. C. "Adapting to a New Generation of College Students." *Thought and Action, The NEA Journal of Higher Education,* Fall 1999, 33–41.

Wang, H., and Grimes, J. W. "A Systematic Approach to Assessing Retention Programs: Identifying Critical Points for Meaningful Interventions and Validating Outcomes Assessment." *Journal of College Student Retention,* 2001, *2*(1), 59–68.

JILLIAN KINZIE *is associate director of the Indiana University Center for Postsecondary Research.*

ROBERT GONYEA *is associate director of the Indiana University Center for Postsecondary Research.*

RICK SHOUP *is a research analyst for the National Survey of Student Engagement at Indiana University Bloomington.*

GEORGE D. KUH *is Chancellor's Professor of Higher Education and director of the Indiana University Center for Postsecondary Research.*

NEW DIRECTIONS FOR TEACHING AND LEARNING • DOI: 10.1002/tl

3

This chapter reports the results of a large study on the effects of part-time faculty on student persistence and suggests that administrators give careful consideration when trying to reduce expenses through the use of such faculty in large beginning courses.

Closing the Gate: Part-Time Faculty Instruction in Gatekeeper Courses and First-Year Persistence

M. Kevin Eagan Jr., Audrey J. Jaeger

Calls for greater accountability in terms of graduation rates and increased economic efficiency among higher education institutions have prompted scholars to examine nontraditional factors that might help to explain the retention puzzle. Terenzini and Reason (2005) emphasize the critical importance of examining factors that lead to first-year student attrition, as four-year institutions, on average, lose more than 25 percent of students by the start of the second year. Recently researchers have begun examining the effects of exposure to part-time faculty on student outcomes (Bettinger and Long, 2006; Jacoby, 2006; Jaeger and Hinz, forthcoming; Jaeger, Thornton, and Eagan, 2007; Kerhberg and Turpin, 2002; Ronco and Cahill, 2006); however, these studies do not specifically address the types of courses students take with part-time faculty. Research on student retention has given limited attention to the role that introductory, or gatekeeper, courses play in students' decisions to remain enrolled at an institution. Gatekeeper courses refer to classes with high enrollment that generally represent the introductory courses required for matriculation into a major field of study (Tobias, 1992).

In this chapter, we describe the employment of part-time faculty in four-year higher education institutions, as well as highlight research on the importance of key gatekeeper courses. Informed by Bean's model (1990) of student attrition, which posits that students leave higher education institutions because of a sense of dissatisfaction with their environment, our analyses

NEW DIRECTIONS FOR TEACHING AND LEARNING, no. 115, Fall 2008   © Wiley Periodicals, Inc.
Published online in Wiley InterScience (www.interscience.wiley.com) • DOI: 10.1002/tl.324

examine how the type of faculty instruction students receive in gatekeeper courses in their first year of college influences their decision to reenroll for the fall of their second year. We draw data from four cohorts of students at four public universities within a state system of higher education. The chapter concludes with implications for administrators and policymakers, as well as directions for future research, in regard to the employment of part-time faculty instructors in gatekeeper courses.

Literature Review

High levels of competition, large class sizes, and high failure rates characterize typical introductory or gatekeeper courses (Tobias, 1992; Van Valkenburg, 1990). Tobias (1990) suggests that professors of these courses generally have high expectations for first-year students and thus teach at a level that supersedes many students' actual abilities. Pedagogical practices of faculty in these courses often encourage passive learning among students as students listen to lectures and take notes rather than engage in discussion with their classmates and instructors (Seymour and Hewitt, 1997). In addition, introductory math and science courses have received significant criticism for grading on a curve and encouraging students to memorize information rather than to think critically about concepts (Seymour and Hewitt, 1997). The competition created by grading on a curve engenders a survival-of-the-fittest mentality among students (Epstein, 2006). Asking questions or otherwise being engaged during class or after the class with the instructor often proves difficult for students in these introductory courses.

Generally introductory science and mathematics courses hold the distinction of gatekeepers (Seymour and Hewitt, 1997; Tobias, 1990). Tobias describes these courses as gatekeepers because, particularly for science, math, and engineering majors, they represent the first class in a series of course work required for matriculation into the major. These gatekeeper courses are designed to weed out students who cannot perform at the expectations of faculty (Seymour and Hewitt, 1997). Gatekeeper courses serve as the initial roadblock to student persistence. Not succeeding in these gatekeeper courses may prompt students, particularly those majoring in math, science, and engineering, to change their major, transfer to a new institution, or drop out of higher education entirely (Seymour, 2001). For students not majoring in math, science, or engineering, gatekeeper courses often come in the form of a general education requirement, and failing to do well in such a course may result in a student's withdrawing from the institution due to an inability to complete required courses necessary to demonstrate degree progress. In addition, poor performance in gatekeeper courses may discourage students psychologically by deflating their self-confidence in their ability to succeed academically (Seymour, 2001).

Given the strong influence of academic engagement on a student's likelihood to persist, having a sense of connection to peers and faculty within gatekeeper courses may substantially bear on a student's decision to reenroll at the same institution. Institutions rely on these high-enrollment introductory courses as a way to improve economic efficiency without much of an understanding of how these types of courses affect student learning and matriculation toward a degree. Prior research that has examined the effect of gatekeeper courses on student retention, academic achievement, and engagement has not considered the type of faculty to whom students have been exposed while taking such classes.

Contingent or contract faculty represent the majority of newly hired academics and nearly half of all faculty at colleges (American Association of University Professors, 2006; Schuster and Finkelstein, 2006). The term *contingent faculty* refers to graduate assistants, postdoctoral researchers, and other types of faculty who are not on the tenure track. In 2003, degree-granting institutions nationwide employed 46.3 percent of faculty in part-time appointments compared to 35.1 percent of faculty in tenured or tenure-track appointments (American Association of University Professors, 2006). Scholars have documented the multitude of reasons that universities tend to employ more part-time faculty, including that these faculty are as much as 80 percent less expensive than full-time faculty (Bettinger and Long, 2006; Gappa, 1984; Leslie, 1998; Liu and Zhang, 2007; Schuster and Finkelstein, 2006). As higher education institutions, particularly those in the public sector, continue to face uncertainty in regard to state appropriations and philanthropic donations, part-time faculty offer increased flexibility in budgeting. In addition, the cost of granting tenure has increased with the elimination of mandatory retirement in 1994, which makes employing contingent faculty an even more attractive option for reducing labor costs (Ehrenberg, 2005; Liu and Zhang, 2007).

Employing part-time faculty can also provide a more student-centered approach (Shuster and Finkelstein, 2007), which may be more responsive to diverse student populations, such as students who work full time and attend college part time. Part-time faculty tend to offer universities flexible scheduling options to meet the needs of students who may need to take classes in late evenings and on weekends. Yet this more flexible response approach to delivering instruction may be at a cost to students. A growing body of research examines the cost to students of substituting tenure-track faculty with part-time and full-time tenure-ineligible faculty.

Many full-time tenure-ineligible faculty are dedicated teachers who, without research expectations placed on them, can more fully commit to teaching (Ehrenberg, 2005). Yet full-time nontenure-track faculty teaching loads are often higher than tenure-track faculty teaching loads, which may leave these faculty with less, rather than more, time for individual students. In contrast, unlike their full-time, tenure-ineligible counterparts, many part-time faculty members are employed at multiple institutions or have jobs outside academia and thus have limited time to meet with students outside class. Schuster (2003) suggests that part-time faculty are less accessible to students, bring less scholarly authority to their jobs, and are less integrated into the campus culture.

Umbach (2007) focused on the relationship between faculty appointments and teaching effectiveness and found that part-time faculty spent less time preparing for class, had fewer interactions with students on course- and noncourse-related issues, challenged their students less, and used active and collaborative teaching techniques less often when compared to their tenured, tenure-track, and tenure-ineligible full-time colleagues. This research also showed a difference in part-time faculty and student interaction across institutional types, with interactions being lowest at research institutions.

A number of single-institution studies have examined the effect of taking courses with part-time faculty on student persistence, but these studies have not specifically focused on faculty teaching gatekeeper courses. The studies consistently have found a significant negative correlation between the amount of exposure to part-time faculty, as measured by percentage of total credits taken with part-time instructors, and students' likelihood of being retained at the institution (Harrington and Schibik, 2004; Jaeger and Hinz, forthcoming; Jaeger, Thornton, and Eagan, 2007; Ronco and Cahill, 2006). Ronco and Cahill (2006) examined students at a public research-intensive university and found a significant, negative effect on retention from having high exposure to part-time faculty instruction. In a similar single-institution study, Jaeger and Hinz (forthcoming) concluded that students' likelihood of being retained significantly decreased as their exposure to part-time faculty instruction increased. Ehrenberg and Zhang (2005) found that increased part-time faculty employment at a four-year institution was negatively associated with student graduation rates. While this study was informative, it focused solely on institutional characteristics and thus did not examine student-level differences. Furthermore, their study did not link specific faculty types with students' courses, which prevented conclusions regarding how exposure to part-time faculty in various courses affected students individually. Examining the relationship between part-time faculty in key introductory courses and student retention is warranted, given the importance of gatekeeper courses and the differential effects that different types of faculty have on student outcomes.

Conceptual Model

The conceptual model for our study assumes that students exposed to greater levels of part-time faculty instruction in introductory courses experience fewer meaningful interactions with those faculty and thus become less integrated into the campus academic culture. Students may view part-time faculty as less stable or less secure, thus becoming less likely to develop relationships with these individuals and see them as role models or potential mentors (Baldwin and Chronister, 2001). Research (Cotten and Wilson, 2006; Endo and Harpel, 1982; Pascarella and Terenzini, 2005) has consistently found a significant and positive relationship between student-faculty interactions and students making gains in a variety of outcomes, even after controlling for key background characteristics. For example, students gain in their cognitive and affective development by increasing their in- and out-of-class interactions with faculty (Endo and Harpel, 1982; Milem and Berger, 1997). Cotten and Wilson (2006) concluded that more frequent interactions with faculty increase students' level of academic achievement in college. In addition, Cotten and Wilson found a positive association between student-faculty interactions and student satisfaction with their overall college experience.

Bean (1990) suggests that increased satisfaction with the overall college experience provides students with reason to persist in college; conversely, Bean suggests that dissatisfaction with college leads to an increased likelihood of attrition. To the extent that prior research suggests a variety of positive outcomes associated with increased student-faculty interactions, it is plausible that students who interact with faculty less often or have fewer meaningful connections to their professors may become dissatisfied with their experience and thus more inclined to leave their college or university. Indeed Jaasma and Koper (2002) note that students who are more satisfied with their experience indicate their instructors are more accessible and involved. Given the limited availability and accessibility of part-time faculty, students likely interact and connect with these instructors less often than with full-time professors, and as a consequence, students may become dissatisfied with their college experience and leave the institution. With this assumption in mind, this study addresses the following research question: Controlling for student background and college-entry characteristics, what is the effect of exposure to contingent faculty instruction in introductory courses on students' decision to persist into the second year?

Methods

We analyzed data from four public universities within a state system of higher education located in the southeastern United States. The Carnegie Foundation for the Advancement of Teaching (2006) classifies these four institutions as four-year, primarily residential institutions. The final sample contained 15,142 students from a doctoral-extensive institution, 13,588 students from two doctoral-intensive institutions, and 2,000 students from a master's comprehensive institution.

Independent variables for the analysis were drawn from enrollment and transcript data. Enrollment data included students' race, gender, Standardized Aptitude Test (SAT) scores, high school grade point average (GPA), state residency, demonstrated financial need, and financial aid awards, including the amount of money students received in the form of loans, grants, and work study.

Transcript data provided information on students' major, first-year course work, and academic performance in each course taken during the first year of enrollment. We classified students' academic majors into five broad categories: humanities; social sciences; life and medical sciences; physics, math, and engineering; and business. In the analyses, undeclared majors were the reference group. Data from students' transcripts were used to derive students' cumulative GPA through the end of the first year.

The transcript data also provided important information regarding the characteristics of the courses in which students enrolled. Drawing from prior research describing various characteristics of gatekeeper courses (Borden and Burton, 1999; Seymour and Hewitt, 1997; Tobias, 1990, 1992; Van Valkenberg, 1990), we defined gatekeeper courses as classes with at least ninety students. In addition, gatekeeper courses in this study were defined as the first (fall semester) or second (spring semester) course in a specific sequence of classes required for a major or general education requirement. These parameters limited the courses in this study considered to be gatekeeper courses to classes in the fields of chemistry, biology, physics, mathematics, engineering, economics, sociology, and psychology.

With gatekeeper courses identified, we calculated the percentage of students' exposure to three types of contingent faculty for their introductory course work. These variables were calculated as the number of introductory course credits taken with three types of contingent faculty (graduate assistants; other part-time faculty, including postdoctoral researchers, adjunct professors, and part-time lecturers; and full-time, tenure-ineligible faculty) divided by the total number of introductory course credits taken for the first year. The term *other part-time faculty* refers to instructors who were employed at or below 0.98 full-time equivalent by the institution and were not classified as graduate assistants. Examples of part-time faculty are part-time lecturers and adjunct professors.

In addition, we calculated the average gatekeeper class size for each student. We constructed this variable by averaging the total number of students in each class for all gatekeeper courses in which a student enrolled during his or her first year. This served as a control variable to account for the contextual effects associated with these large, competitive classroom environments and allowed us to determine how exposure to contingent faculty affected students' likelihood of being retained into the second year, independent of the average number of students in their key gatekeeper courses.

Finally, the analyses controlled for the number of gatekeeper credits a student completed during his or her first year. Controlling for the number of gatekeeper credits, rather than the total number of credits completed in the first year, enabled us to isolate the effects of exposure to various types of faculty within these key introductory courses.

This study employed separate logistic regressions for each Carnegie classification (one doctoral-extensive university, two doctoral-intensive universities, and one master's comprehensive university) to examine the effects of contingent faculty exposure in introductory courses on students' likelihood to persist.

NEW DIRECTIONS FOR TEACHING AND LEARNING • DOI: 10.1002/tl

Table 3.1. Descriptive Statistics by Institutional Type

	Doctoral Extensive		Doctoral Intensive		Master's Comprehensive	
	Mean	SD	Mean	SD	Mean	SD
Retained to second fall semester	0.90	0.30	0.76	0.42	0.88	0.33
Black	0.10	0.30	0.15	0.36	0.02	0.15
Asian	0.04	0.20	0.04	0.20	0.02	0.13
Hispanic	0.02	0.15	0.02	0.15	0.02	0.13
American Indian	0.01	0.09	0.00	0.07	0.01	0.07
Other race	0.01	0.12	0.02	0.15	0.03	0.16
White	0.81	0.39	0.76	0.43	0.90	0.34
Female	0.44	0.50	0.61	0.49	0.51	0.50
Out-of-state resident	0.10	0.15	0.11	0.05	0.10	0.30
High school GPA	3.59	0.26	3.49	0.40	0.35	0.29
Combined SAT	11.91	1.24	10.60	1.26	11.23	1.12
Humanities	0.05	0.22	0.11	0.31	0.11	0.32
Social sciences	0.12	0.32	0.22	0.41	0.35	0.48
Life and medical sciences	0.16	0.36	0.13	0.33	0.11	0.31
Physics, math, and engineering	0.38	0.49	0.09	0.29	0.06	0.23
Business	0.07	0.26	0.11	0.31	0.10	0.30
Undeclared	0.22	0.15	0.34	0.25	0.27	0.21
Need	3.44	5.42	4.10	5.44	2.71	5.85
Grants	3.31	4.85	1.82	2.79	1.50	2.53
Subsidized loans	0.57	1.17	0.95	1.67	0.67	1.24
Work study	0.06	0.26	0.08	0.49	0.08	0.38
Total first-year GPA	2.72	0.80	2.57	0.89	2.74	0.80
Percentage of introductory courses with graduate students	0.08	0.20	0.05	0.20	0.00	0.00
Percentage of introductory courses with other part-time faculty	0.22	0.28	0.08	0.29	0.14	0.32
Total introductory credits earned in first year	9.53	4.28	5.12	2.51	4.74	2.23
Average class size in gatekeeper courses	180.48	84.12	172.12	83.10	125.64	49.26

Table 3.1 presents descriptive statistics of the variables in the analysis. First-year retention rates ranged from 76 percent at the doctoral-intensive universities to 90 percent at the doctoral-extensive university. Exposure to graduate assistant instruction in gatekeeper courses appeared to be relatively low across all institutional types, as students, on average, had less than 10 percent of their introductory credits with graduate assistant instructors. Specifically, at the master's comprehensive institution, no graduate students taught courses identified as gatekeeper ones. Students at the doctoral-extensive institution had nearly 25 percent of all of their gatekeeper credits with other types of part-time faculty, whereas students at the doctoral-intensive institutions had just 8 percent of introductory credits with such faculty.

NEW DIRECTIONS FOR TEACHING AND LEARNING • DOI: 10.1002/tl

Student financial need ranged from an average of $3,440 at the doctoral-extensive institution to $4,100 at the doctoral-intensive institutions. More students (34 percent) at the master's comprehensive institutions had not declared a major by the end of their first year compared to students at the other types of institutions. The doctoral-extensive institution holds a strong national reputation for its engineering program and therefore had a high concentration (38 percent) of physics, math, and engineering majors.

As anticipated, average gatekeeper class sizes were largest at the doctoral-extensive institution and smallest at the master's comprehensive institution. Similarly, students at the doctoral-extensive institution tended to have more credits in gatekeeper courses compared to their peers at the doctoral-intensive and master's comprehensive institutions. Finally, though not shown in Table 3.1, it is important to note that 97 percent of first-year students at the doctoral-extensive institution had enrolled in at least one gatekeeper course. In contrast, 71 percent of students at the doctoral-intensive and just 18 percent of students at the master's comprehensive institutions had enrolled in a gatekeeper course during their first year.

Table 3.2 presents the results of the logistical regression, presented as odds ratios. Odds ratios greater than 1 indicate an increased likelihood of persistence into the second year, whereas odds ratios less than 1 suggest reduced odds of persistence. The results suggest that students, regardless of institutional type, were not significantly affected by exposure to graduate student instruction in their introductory course work. The graduate student exposure variable was dropped from the model for students at the master's comprehensive institution, as no graduate students instructed gatekeeper courses at this university. Similarly, students appeared not to be significantly affected by exposure to full-time, tenure-ineligible faculty. Initial analyses suggested multicollinearity associated with the full-time, tenure-ineligible faculty variable. Due to this multicollinearity and its nonsignificance in initial models, we dropped the full-time, tenure-ineligible variable from future analyses.

Regarding other types of part-time faculty, such as postdoctoral researchers, adjunct professors, and part-time lecturers, in gatekeeper courses, students became less likely to persist into their second year as their exposure to such part-time faculty increased. In each institutional type, the effect of exposure to other part-time faculty was negative. Among the doctoral-extensive and -intensive institutions, students were about 20 percent less likely (odds ratio = 0.80, $p < 0.05$) to persist into the second year for every percentage point increase in exposure to other part-time faculty in gatekeeper courses. The effect at the master's comprehensive institution was slightly stronger: students became about 37 percent (odds ratio = 0.63, $p < 0.05$) less likely to be retained into the second year for every percentage point increase in exposure to other part-time faculty in gatekeeper courses.

Another clear trend across all institutional types, albeit less substantial, was the significant and negative effect of average gatekeeper class size on students' likelihood of persistence. As the average class size in gatekeeper

Table 3.2. Logistic Regression Results by Institutional Type

Variable	Doctoral Extensive			Doctoral Intensive			Masters Comprehensive		
	Odds Ratio	SE	Significance	Odds Ratio	SE	Significance	Odds Ratio	SE	Significance
Black	1.77	0.12	***	1.66	0.09	***	1.26	0.51	
Asian	1.14	0.16		1.56	0.14	***	1.05	0.59	
Hispanic	1.05	0.20		1.17	0.17		1.00	0.56	
American Indian	0.81	0.33		0.96	0.32		0.43	0.72	
Other race	0.89	0.23		0.79	0.17		1.34	0.51	
Female	0.76	0.07	***	0.84	0.06	***	0.80	0.16	
Out-of-state resident	0.45	0.09	***	0.52	0.08	***	0.55	0.24	*
High school GPA	0.94	0.08		0.75	0.06	***	1.00	0.19	
Combined SAT	0.89	0.02	***	0.96	0.02	*	0.99	0.05	*
Humanities	1.03	0.14		1.08	0.10		1.04	0.25	
Social sciences	0.95	0.10		1.31	0.07	***	1.08	0.19	
Life and medical sciences	0.81	0.10	*	0.96	0.08		1.00	0.28	
Physics, math, and engineering	1.18	0.09	*	1.39	0.11	**	1.34	0.38	
Business	2.35	0.15	***	0.95	0.09		0.80	0.26	
Need	0.98	0.01		0.97	0.01	***	1.00	0.02	
Grants	1.02	0.01	*	1.08	0.01	***	1.03	0.04	
Subsidized loans	0.98	0.04		1.01	0.02		0.91	0.07	
Work study	1.25	0.14		0.96	0.05		0.90	0.20	
Total first-year GPA	3.16	0.04	***	3.33	0.03	***	2.10	0.09	***
Percentage of introductory courses with graduate students	0.82	0.15		0.79	0.13				
Percentage of introductory courses with other part-time faculty	0.80	0.11	*	0.80	0.09	**	0.63	0.23	*
Total gatekeeper credits completed in first year	1.25	0.01	***	1.34	0.02	***	1.35	0.05	***
Average class size in gatekeeper courses	0.97	0.01	***	0.94	0.01	***	0.92	0.01	***
Percentage correctly classified	74.70			73.30			69.30		
Hosmer and Lemeshow chi-square statistic	121.13		***	174.82		***	45.87		***

Note: ***$p < 0.001$. **$p < 0.01$. *$p < 0.05$.

courses increased, students became significantly less likely to persist into their second year. This trend was weakest at the doctoral-extensive institution (odds ratio = 0.97, $p < 0.001$) and strongest, although still modest, at the master's comprehensive institution (odds ratio = 0.92, $p < 0.001$).

As the number of gatekeeper credits that students completed increased, their likelihood of persistence also increased. This variable served as a proxy for students' level of academic engagement, or enrollment intensity, during their first year. Students at the doctoral-extensive institution became about 25 percent more likely (odds ratio = 1.25, $p < 0.001$) to persist for every additional gatekeeper credit they completed. Similarly, students at the master's comprehensive institution became about 35 percent more likely (odds ratio = 1.35, $p < 0.001$) to persist for every additional gatekeeper credit they completed. This result may suggest that students who attempt more hours may have a greater sense of self-efficacy and are already more likely to persist.

Consistent with prior research (Titus, 2006), students' cumulative first-year GPA had a significant positive effect on persistence likelihood, as students at the doctoral-extensive (odds ratio = 3.16, $p < 0.001$) and doctoral-intensive (odds ratio = 3.33, $p < 0.001$) institutions became more than three times as likely to persist for every unit increase in GPA. Students at the master's comprehensive institution became more than twice as likely to persist for every unit gain in first-year college GPA (odds ratio = 2.10, $p < 0.001$).

Students from out of state had significantly reduced odds of persistence than their in-state peers across all institutional types. In general, students from out of state were about half as likely to return for their second year compared to their in-state classmates. The state system to which the institutions in this study belong limits the proportion of out-of-state students the institutions can enroll each year. During the time frame of this study, that limit was 17 percent.

The models for each institutional type did a fair job at correctly classifying each case in the analysis as persisting or not persisting. The poorest-predicting model was the model for the master's comprehensive institution, which correctly classified 69 percent of all cases. The models for the doctoral-extensive and doctoral-intensive institutions correctly classified 75 percent and 73 percent of cases, respectively.

Implications and Conclusions

The results from our study have several implications for higher education administrators and policymakers who face the task of balancing the financial reality of needing to employ greater numbers of part-time faculty while simultaneously maintaining, if not raising, retention and graduation rates. First, students appeared not to be significantly affected by having graduate students as instructors for their introductory course work. Second, exposure to full-time, tenure-ineligible faculty did not appear to significantly affect students' likelihood of persisting into their second year. Perhaps the fact that

NEW DIRECTIONS FOR TEACHING AND LEARNING • DOI: 10.1002/tl

graduate students and full-time, tenure-ineligible faculty tend to be more visible and more integrated into the campus culture mitigates any shortcomings they may have in course preparation or pedagogical expertise. In addition, Umbach (2007) concluded that full-time, tenure-ineligible faculty behaved more like their full-time, tenure-eligible colleagues and less like their part-time counterparts. The nonsignificant finding for exposure to full-time, tenure-ineligible faculty on first-year student persistence seems to support Umbach's conclusion (2007), at least in part. Because our data did not provide specific information about faculty practices inside and outside the classroom, future research would need to examine specifically how the actual behaviors and pedagogical practices of full-time, tenure-ineligible faculty affect students on a variety of outcomes and compare these practices to those of tenured and tenure-track faculty.

Third, students appear to be significantly and negatively affected by having gatekeeper courses taught by other part-time faculty. This finding emerges even after controlling for key variables, such as students' prior and current academic achievement, academic major, average gatekeeper course size, and number of gatekeeper credits a student completed. By controlling for these extenuating variables, we see that exposure to other part-time faculty may have less to do with this faculty subgroup's pedagogy and possibly more to do with their level of availability and accessibility on campus. According to Seymour and Hewitt (1997), these gatekeeper courses are characterized by high enrollments and high levels of competition among students. Because of these characteristics, gatekeeper courses suffer from poor pedagogical practices regardless of the type of instructor, as these classes generally focus on lectures and fail to engage students in the classroom. Given that Schuster (2003) and Schuster and Finkelstein (2006) concluded that part-time faculty are generally less accessible and less available to students, it is possible that the negative effects on retention of having gatekeeper classes taught by other part-time faculty stemmed from students' inability to meet with or connect with these instructors outside the classroom for additional guidance or assistance with course content. In fact, the type of interaction that students report as being most important is contact with faculty outside the classroom (Stodt, 1987). Furthermore, students' perceptions of faculty members' availability and concern for them have positive and significant effects on persistence (Halpin, 1990; Mallette and Cabrera, 1991). Haeger (1998) notes that part-time faculty often do not have offices, hold limited or no meeting hours, have limited or no telephone and computer access, and are not compensated for advising students. Thus, part-time faculty may not be as engaged with students outside the classroom, leading students to conclude that this faculty subgroup has a lack of interest in interacting with them. Since gatekeeper courses are often the most challenging classes for first-year students, the ability to connect with faculty outside the classroom may be an important component to students' pursuit of success.

Student success should be the force that drives institutional decision making. Although research suggests that the employment of part-time faculty instructors enables institutions to become more cost-efficient with their academic labor (Bettinger and Long, 2006; Gappa, 1984; Leslie, 1998; Liu and Zhang, 2007; Schuster and Finkelstein, 2006), this financial flexibility may be at a significant cost to an institution's ability to retain students. If students are unsuccessful in navigating foundational high-enrollment introductory courses because of the type of faculty instructing such courses, administrators should reconsider the types of courses that part-time faculty teach. Perhaps relying more heavily on full-time tenured faculty, who likely have a stronger presence on the campus and may maintain a stronger sense of availability to students, to teach these key gatekeeper courses may serve as a feasible alternative to having part-time instructors take on these important responsibilities. Hagedorn, Perrakis, and Maxwell (2002) concluded that to encourage student success, colleges should not rely heavily on part-time faculty who hold sparse office hours and appear inaccessible. Bean (2005) notes, "When students feel faculty members do not care about the student's development, their bonds to the institution weaken" (p. 225).

The finding of negative effects on persistence from the large class sizes in these key introductory courses supports prior research (Borden and Burton, 1999; Seymour and Hewitt, 1997). Kennedy and Siegfried (1997) noted that small-class discussion methods are favored when instructors hope to instill skills such as retention of information, problem solving, critical thinking, and attitude change or motivation in students. Because of the difficulty in creating collaborative curricula for high-enrollment classes, instructors, regardless of level of appointment, may rely more heavily on lecture to teach students the content. The lack of interaction between students and instructor in the classroom may lead to increased disengagement among students, which translates into a decreased likelihood of persistence (Bean, 1990). This disengagement in students' academic lives may contribute to students' sense of dissatisfaction with their environment, which can lead to an increased risk of attrition (Bean, 1990). Similarly, in a qualitative study addressing college graduates' perceptions relative to what facilitated their continued enrollment, Hofmann, Posteraro, and Presz (1994) found that graduates noted that faculty were the primary way in which the college contributed to their success. In addition, an important feature to their success was small class size. This conclusion is critical to note as it illustrates students' perceived benefits of faculty-student interaction and small class size.

Future research needs to address how the level of availability and the pedagogical practices of various types of contingent faculty in gatekeeper courses affect students' likelihood to persist. While we appropriately controlled for key intervening variables, such as student major, course size, and enrollment intensity, we were unable to account for the level of availability and pedagogical practices employed by various faculty types. Given that prior research (Schuster and Finkelstein, 2006; Umbach, 2007) suggests that full-time tenure-ineligible faculty are significantly different from their part-time counterparts across several dimensions, future research using advanced statistical techniques, such as hierarchical linear modeling, needs to examine how these specific characteristics of contingent faculty intersect with and affect student experiences and outcomes.

Given the consistent findings from this study as well as previous related studies (Harrington and Schibik, 2004; Jaeger and Hinz, forthcoming; Ronco and Cahill, 2006) and the increasing reliance on part-time faculty labor, particularly in the public sector, administrators and policymakers need to revisit their current practices with regard to part-time faculty. The use of part-time faculty has become a fiscal reality; however, administrators can become more intentional about the placement of part-time instructors in specific courses. Rather than appointing part-time instructors to teach important foundational courses for lower-division undergraduates, perhaps these instructors would be better suited to teach courses with more advanced students who have established a greater sense of commitment to their institution and degree program. If the negative effects of part-time faculty exposure on first-year student retention continue to be ignored within institutions of higher education, these institutions may continue to sacrifice their ability to retain students in order to remain cost-efficient.

References

American Association of University Professors. *AAUP Contingent Faculty Index.* Washington, D.C.: American Association of University Professors, 2006. Retrieved Dec. 14, 2006, from www.aaup.org/AAUP/issues/contingent/.

Baldwin, R. G., and Chronister, J. L. *Teaching Without Tenure: Policies and Practices for a New Era.* Baltimore, Md.: Johns Hopkins University Press, 2001.

Bean, J. P. "Why Students Leave: Insights from Research." In D. Hossler and J. P. Bean (eds.), *The Strategic Management of College Enrollments.* San Francisco: Jossey-Bass, 1990.

Bean, J. P. "Nine Themes of College Student Retention." In A. Seidman (ed.), *College Student Retention.* Westport, Conn.: Praeger, 2005.

Bettinger, E. P., and Long B. T. "The Increasing Use of Adjunct Instructors at Public Institutions: Are We Hurting Students?" In R. G. Ehrenbert (ed.), *What's Happening to Public Higher Education.* Westport, Conn.: Praeger, 2006.

Borden, V.M.H., and Burton, K. L. "The Impact of Class Size on Student Performance in Introductory Courses." Paper presented at the Annual Forum of the Association for Institutional Research, Seattle, Wash., May 1999. (ED 433 782)

Carnegie Foundation for the Advancement of Teaching. *Classification Descriptions.* 2006. Retrieved Apr. 1, 2007, from http://www.carnegiefoundation.org/classifications/index.asp?key=785.

Cotten, S. R., and Wilson, B. "Student-Faculty Interactions: Dynamics and Determinants." *Higher Education,* 2006, *51,* 487–519.

Ehrenberg, R. G. *The Changing Nature of the Faculty and Faculty Employment Practices.* Ithaca, N.Y.: Cornell Higher Education Research Institute, 2005. Retrieved Dec. 30, 2007, from www.ilr.cornell.edu/cheri/wp/cheri_wp78.pdf.

Ehrenberg, R. G., and Zhang, L. "Do Tenure and Tenure-Track Faculty Matter?" *Journal of Human Resources,* 2005, *40,* 647–659.

Endo, J. J., and Harpel, R. L. "The Effect of Student-Faculty Interaction on Students' Educational Outcomes." *Research in Higher Education,* 1982, *16*(2), 115–138.

Epstein, D. "So That's Why They're Leaving." *Inside Higher Education,* July 26, 2006.
Retrieved Apr. 15, 2007, from http://insidehighered.com/news/2006/07/26/scipipeline.

Gappa, J. M. *Part-Time Faculty: Higher Education at a Crossroads.* ASHE Report, no. 3,
vol. 10. San Francisco: Jossey-Bass, 1984.

Haeger, J. D. "Part-Time Faculty, Quality Programs, and Economic Realities." In D. W.
Leslie (ed.), *The Growing Use of Part-Time Faculty: Understanding Causes and Effects.*
San Francisco: Jossey-Bass, 1998.

Hagedorn, L., Perrakis, A., and Maxwell, W. *The Negative Commandments: Ten Ways
Community Colleges Hinder Student Success.* 2002. (ED 466 262)

Halpin, R. "An Application of the Tinto Model to the Analysis of Freshman Persistence
in a Community College." *Community College Review,* 1990, *17,* 22–32.

Harrington, C., and Schibik, T. *Caveat Emptor: Is There a Relationship Between Part-Time
Faculty Utilization and Student Learning Outcomes and Retention?* Tallahassee, Fla.:
Association of Institutional Research, 2004.

Hofmann, J. M., Posteraro, C., and Presz, H. A. "Adult Learners: Why Were They Successful? Lessons Learned via an Adult Learner Task Force." Paper presented at the
Adult Learner Task Force Conference, Columbia, S.C., May 1994. (ED 375 269)

Jaasma, M., and Koper, R. "Out-of-Class Communication Between Female and Male Students and Faculty: The Relationship to Student Perceptions of Instructor Immediacy."
Women's Studies in Communication, 2002, *25,* 119–137.

Jacoby, D. "Effects of Part-Time Faculty Employment on Community College Graduation Rates." *Journal of Higher Education,* 2006, *77*(6), 1081–1103.

Jaeger, A. J., and Hinz, D. "The Effects of Part-Time Faculty on First Year Freshman
Retention: A Predictive Model Using Logistic Regression." *Journal of College Student
Retention,* forthcoming.

Jaeger, A. J., Thornton, C. H., and Eagan, K. "Effects of Faculty Type on First Year Student Retention and Performance." Paper presented at the meeting of the Association
for the Study of Higher Education, Louisville, Ky., Nov. 2007.

Kehrberg, N., and Turpin, W. K. "Impact of Part-Time Faculty on Freshman Performance, Satisfaction and Retention." Paper presented at the meeting of the North Carolina Association for Institutional Research, Greensboro, N.C., Mar. 2002.

Kennedy, P. E., and Siegfried, J. J. "Class Size and Achievement in Introductory Economics: Evidence from the TUCE III Data." Economics of Education Review, 1997, 16(4),
385–394.

Leslie, D. W. "The Growing Use of Part-Time Faculty: Understanding Causes and Effects."
In New Directions for Higher Education, no. 104. San Francisco: Jossey-Bass, 1998.

Liu, X., and Zhang, L. *What Determines Employment of Part-Time Faculty in Higher Education Institutions?* Ithaca, N.Y.: Cornell Higher Education Research Institute, 2007.
Retrieved Dec. 30, 2007, from www.ilr.cornell.edu/cheri/wp/cheri_wp105.pdf.

Mallette, B., and Cabrera, A. "Determinants of Withdrawal Behavior: An Exploratory
Study." *Research in Higher Education,* 1991, *32*(2), 179–194.

Milem, J., and Berger, J. "A Modified Model of College Student Persistence: Exploring
the Relationship Between Astin's Theory of Involvement and Tinto's Theory of Student Departure." *Journal of College Student Development,* 1997, *38,* 387–400.

Pascarella, E. T., and Terenzini, P. T. *How College Affects Students: A Third Decade of
Research.* (2nd ed.) San Francisco: Jossey-Bass, 2005.

Ronco, S., and Cahill, J. *Does It Matter Who's in the Classroom? Effect of Instructor Type
on Student Retention, Achievement and Satisfaction.* Tallahassee, Fla.: Association of
Institutional Research, 2006.

Schuster, J. H. (ed.). "The Faculty Makeover: What Does It Mean for Students?" In E. Ben-
jamin (ed.), *Exploring the Role of Contingent Instructional Staff in Undergraduate Learning.* New Directions For Higher Education, no. 123. San Francisco: Jossey-Bass, 2003.

Schuster, J. H., and Finkelstein, M. J. *The American Faculty: The Restructuring of Academic Work and Careers.* Baltimore, Md.: Johns Hopkins University Press, 2006.

Schuster, J. H., and Finkelstein, M. J. *On the Brink: Assessing the Status of American Faculty.* Berkeley: University of California, Berkeley, 2007. Retrieved Jan. 9, 2008, from http://cshe.berkeley.edu/publications/docs/ROP.Schuster.3.07.pdf.

Seymour, E. "Tracking the Processes of Change in US Undergraduate Education in Science, Mathematics, Engineering, and Technology." *Bureau of Sociological Research,* 2001, 86(1), 79–105.

Seymour, E., and Hewitt, N. M. *Talking About Leaving: Why Undergraduates Leave the Sciences.* Boulder, Colo.: Westview Press, 1997.

Stodt, M. M. "Educational Excellence as a Prescription for Retention." In M. McGinty Stodt and W. M. Klepper (eds.), *Increasing Retention: Academic and Student Affairs Administrators in Partnership.* New Directions for Higher Education, no. 60, pp. 5–13. San Francisco: Jossey-Bass, 1987.

Terenzini, P. T., and Reason, R. D. "Parsing the First Year of College: A Conceptual Framework for Studying College Impacts." Paper presented at the meeting of the Association for the Study of Higher Education, Philadelphia, Nov. 2005.

Titus, M. A. "Understanding the Influence of the Financial Context of Institutions on Student Persistence at Four-Year Colleges and Universities." *Journal of Higher Education,* 2006, 77(2), 353–375.

Tobias, S. "Stemming the Science Shortfall at College." In S. Tobias (ed.), *They're Not Dumb, They're Different.* Tucson, Ariz.: Research Corporation, 1990.

Tobias, S. "Science Education Reform: What's Wrong with the Process?" In S. Tobias (ed.), *Revitalizing Undergraduate Science: Why Some Things Works and Most Don't.* Tucson, Ariz.: Research Corporation, 1992.

Umbach, P. D. "How Effective Are They? Exploring the Impact of Contingent Faculty on Undergraduate Education." *Review of Higher Education,* 2007, 30(2), 91–124.

Van Valkenburg, M. "Second Option: Turning Off Students: Our Gatekeeper Courses." *Engineering Education,* 1990, 80(6), 620.

M. KEVIN EAGAN *is a graduate student at the University of California, Los Angeles.*

AUDREY J. JAEGER *is an associate professor of higher education at North Carolina State University*

NEW DIRECTIONS FOR TEACHING AND LEARNING • DOI: 10.1002/tl

4

*The research presented here indicates that exposure to
organized and clear classroom instruction may have
positive net effects on the probability of returning to
an institution for the second year of college.*

Effective Instruction and College Student Persistence: Some New Evidence

Ernest T. Pascarella, Tricia A. Seifert, Elizabeth J. Whitt

An extensive body of correlational and experimental evidence has demonstrated the positive (and perhaps causal) link between different dimensions of effective postsecondary classroom instruction and both course-level learning and more general cognitive growth (for a summary of this research, see Pascarella and Terenzini, 1991, 2005). In this chapter, we present evidence from a longitudinal study of first-year students at a large research university to suggest that overall exposure to organized and clear classroom instruction may also have positive net effects on the probability of returning to an institution for the second year of college.

Effective Classroom Instruction

What constitutes effective classroom instructional practices or teacher behavior in postsecondary education is no longer a black box. Hundreds of correlational investigations have linked student perceptions of teacher behaviors such as instructional clarity, course organization and preparation, teacher expressiveness, and feedback to students to various measures of course-related knowledge acquisition or content mastery. A number of

The research on which this chapter is based was supported by a generous grant from the Office of the Provost to the Center for Research on Undergraduate Education at the University of Iowa.

comprehensive meta-analytic or narrative reviews of this extensive body of research have been conducted (Braskamp and Ory, 1994; Cashin, 1999; d'Apollonia and Abrami, 1997; Feldman, 1997; Greenwald, 1997; Marsh and Dunkin, 1997; McKeachie, 1997). A distillation of these reviews (Pascarella, 2006) suggests three general conclusions about student perceptions of teacher classroom behaviors or instructional practices: (1) these perceptions are multi-dimensional, (2) they are reasonably reliable and stable, and (3) they have moderate positive correlations (for example, .30 to .50) with various measures of course learning such as course grade and course final examination.

Evidence on the validity of student perceptions of teaching is not limited to correlational investigations. Three of the dimensions of student perceptions of teaching with the strongest links to course achievement in correlational research—instructional clarity (clear explanations, effective use of examples), organization/preparation (effective use of class time, use of course objectives), and expressiveness (speaking emphatically, eye contact)—have been demonstrated with experiments (Hines, Cruickshank, and Kennedy, 1985; Schonwetter, Menec, and Perry, 1995; Schonwetter, Perry, and Struthers, 1994; Wood and Murray, 1999).

Although nearly all the research on student perceptions of teaching focuses on their link to specific course achievement, at least some evidence suggests that instructional organization, or a combination of instructional organization and clarity, might have positive impacts on more general academic competencies or skills not directly tied to a specific course. A group of researchers affiliated with the National Study of Student Learning (Pascarella and others, 1996) developed two five-item scales, termed instructional organization/preparation and instructional skill/clarity, that appropriated specific items appearing in previous research (Cohen, 1981; Feldman, 1989, 1994). Organization/preparation had constituent items such as "presentation of material is well organized" and "class time is used effectively" and had an alpha reliability of .87. Skill/clarity had constituent items such as "instructors give clear explanations" and "instructors make good use of examples to get across difficult points," with an alpha reliability of .86. In a series of longitudinal investigations with samples from eighteen diverse institutions, the researchers found that the more students reported that the overall instruction they received in college was high on the organization/preparation scale, the greater their gains were on standardized measures of critical thinking, reading comprehension, and mathematics. These significant, positive associations persisted even after statistical controls were introduced for an extensive array of confounding influences, including precollege cognitive test scores, sex, race, academic motivation, full- or part-time enrollment, and patterns of specific types of coursework taken (Pascarella and others, 1996; Edison, Doyle, and Pascarella, 1998; Whitt and others, 2003). The failure of the instructional skill/clarity scale to also show significant, positive net associations with cognitive gains was in all likelihood due to its high correlation with the organization/preparation scale (.73). In other words, overall collegiate instruction seen by students as high in organization/preparation was also seen by students as high in skill/clarity. Indeed a recent investigation that combined the two scales into a ten-item measure of student perceptions of organization and clarity in overall instruction during college (alpha = .89) found that the resultant composite scale had a net positive influence on gains on a measure of reading comprehension over three years of college (Bray, Pascarella, and Pierson, 2004).

Evidence does exist to suggest that student perceptions of teaching can be influenced by a number of extraneous course characteristics such as expected or actual course grade (Krautmann and Sander, 1999), academic discipline (Murray, Jelley, and Renaud, 1996), class size (Wachtel, 1998), and grading leniency (Greenwald and Gillmore, 1997). These extraneous influences may complicate matters when student perceptions of teaching are employed in faculty promotion or salary decisions. As Aleamoni (1999) suggested, however, this probably does not seriously detract from the usefulness of student perceptions of teaching in identifying classroom instructional practices that enhance course learning.

Exposure to Effective Instruction and College Persistence

A number of scholars have hypothesized that the nature and quality of classroom instruction may not only influence learning outcomes, but might also play a significant role in student decisions to persist at, or depart from, a particular college or university (Braxton, Hirschy, and McClendon, 2004; Braxton and McClendon, 2001–2002; Braxton and Mundy, 2001–2002; Tinto, 2006–2007). Indeed, a small body of evidence tends to support this hypothesis (Braxton, Bray, and Berger, 2000; Braxton, Milem, and Sullivan, 2000; Nora, Cabrera, Hagedorn, and Pascarella, 1996; Tinto, 1997). While most of this research has considered the effects of different classroom pedagogical approaches such as active or cooperative learning, the study by Braxton, Bray, and Berger (2000) considered the impact of specific teacher behaviors most directly. Guided by Tinto's conceptual model (1975, 1993) as framework for their study, Braxton, Bray, and Berger hypothesized that students exposed to faculty members who exhibit instructional organization and clarity in their classes frequently might be more confident and relaxed about their academic achievement. Thus, they might perceive that they have more time "to invest the psychological energy necessary to establish membership in the social communities of their college or university" (Braxton, Bray, and Berger, 2000, p. 216). Increased social integration, in turn, would enhance institutional commitment and intent to persist at the institution. Using measures of overall instructional organization and clarity essentially the same as Pascarella and others (1996), their findings were quite consistent with their hypotheses. Net of important confounding influences, overall exposure to organized and clear instruction enhanced both a measure of student social integration and reported intent to reenroll at an institution for the second year of college.

The study we summarize in the rest of this chapter builds on and extends the work of Braxton, Bray, and Berger (2000). It follows a sample of students beyond the end of the first year of college to determine if overall exposure to organized and clear classroom instruction increases the net probability of actual reenrollment at an institution for the second year of college.

Study Methods

In this section we briefly describe the study methods in terms of the guiding analytical model, institution and sample, study design, variables, and data analyses.

Analytical Model. The analytical model guiding the study was based on an extensive body of research evidence and is illustrated in Figures 4.1 and 4.2. (For a synthesis of this body of evidence, see sources such as Braxton, Hirschy, and McClendon, 2004; Goodman and Pascarella, 2006; Pascarella and Terenzini, 2005; and Tinto, 1993.) Figure 4.1 models the hypothesized total effect of effective classroom instruction (defined as organization and clarity) on persistence into the second year of college (the student reenrolled for the second year of postsecondary education at the study institution). The model assumes that persistence is a function not only of exposure to effective classroom instruction, but also of student background characteristics and tested academic preparation, as well as other college experiences. This set of variables includes such influences as race, sex, family social origins, and standardized test scores (for example, the ACT or

Figure 4.1. Total Effects Model

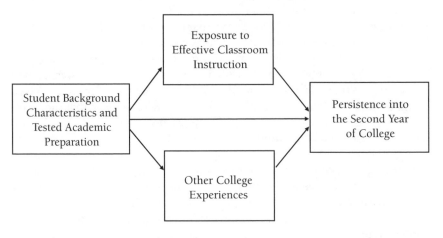

SAT). Other college experiences include such factors as financial aid, work during college, place of residence, and a range of social and academic involvements such as Greek affiliation, living-learning or honors programs, campus leadership positions, social drinking, attending on-campus lectures, and intramural sports. According to the conceptual model shown in Figure 4.1, we anticipated that with statistical controls in place for student background characteristics, precollege test scores, and other college experiences, overall exposure to organized and clear instruction during the first year of college would have a significant, positive total effect on the probability of enrolling for the second year of college (Alwin and Hauser, 1975).

The hypothesized indirect effects of exposure to organized and clear classroom instruction on persistence are modeled in Figure 4.2. According to this conceptual model, we anticipated that when measures of cumulative college grades, satisfaction with the education being received, and educational degree plans were added to the total effects model (Figure 4.1), two things would happen. First, net of all other influences, cumulative first-year grades, satisfaction with college, and degree plans would have a positive influence on persistence; and second, the direct positive influence of organized and clear instruction on persistence would become small and nonsignificant. This would indicate a positive indirect effect of overall organized and clear instruction on persistence, mediated through the positive effects of organized and clear instruction on cumulative grades, satisfaction with the education being received, and degree plans (Alwin and Hauser, 1975; Pascarella, 2006). We reasoned that if organized and clear instruction at the course level improved course-level learning, then overall exposure to organized and clear instruction would enhance cumulative academic achievement in college. We also hypothesized that exposure to effective instruction would have an affective dimension manifest in higher levels of student satisfaction with their undergraduate education. Finally, based on recent evidence that overall exposure to organized and clear instruction is positively linked to increases in educational aspirations (Pascarella, Wolniak, Pierson, and Flowers, 2004), we anticipated that the same relationship would exist in our sample.

Institution and Sample. The study was carried out at a large (thirty thousand students) public, primarily residential research university located in a small midwestern city. The institution is a member of the Association of American Universities and has a strong graduate and professional school emphasis, as well as a large undergraduate program. The sample consisted of 1,353 first-year students, about one-third of the first-year class enrolled at the institution. Although the sample was representative of the population of first-year students by race/ethnicity, women and individuals with higher ACT scores were overrepresented. To adjust for this bias, an algorithm was developed to weight the sample up to population values by sex and ACT composite score.

Study Design. The design of the study was longitudinal: data were collected at four points in time. The first data collection was prior to the

Figure 4.2. Direct and Indirect Effects Model

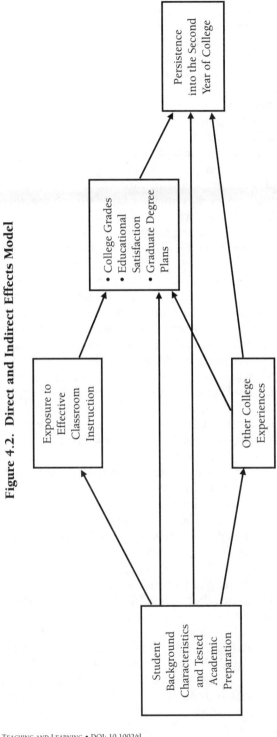

students' enrollment at the institution in late August 2005 and included demographic background characteristics and a standardized measure of academic preparation. The second data collection was during late March 2006, about the middle of the second semester of the students' first year of college. This data collection was in the form of a Web-based survey instrument that took about thirty minutes to complete. The survey collected data on demographic and background characteristics and extensive information on student college experiences and their engagement in a variety of activities and programs. The Web-based survey also asked students about their degree of satisfaction with the education they were receiving at the institution and their intended highest educational degree. The third data collection occurred during summer 2006 and consisted of student first-year cumulative grade point average (GPA). Finally, the fourth data collection point was early fall 2006, at which time we determined whether each of the students in the sample had reenrolled at the study institution.

Background Characteristics and Tested Academic Preparation. Student background characteristics consisted of sex, race/ethnicity, father's educational degree attainment, and mother's educational degree attainment. The ACT composite score (or its SAT equivalent) was used to test academic preparation. Sex, race, and ACT composite score were obtained from official university records held by the office of the university registrar. Father's and mother's levels of formal education were obtained from the survey. We did not use high school grades in the study because we were using first-year college grades in the analyses and wanted to avoid the interpretative problem of collinearity between the two variables.

Other College Experiences. The Web-based survey instrument collected extensive information on student first-year experiences in college other than exposure to effective instruction. These other first-year experiences included such factors as receipt of financial aid; hours per week of on- or off-campus work; first-year place of residence (fraternity or sorority house, off campus within three miles from campus, and off campus farther than three miles from campus versus campus housing); intended academic major (arts and humanities, education, engineering, journalism/communications, natural sciences, social sciences, nursing, and other versus business); and reported alcohol use during a typical two-week period. Also included as other college experiences was whether students participated in any of thirteen different experiences, including university-sponsored programs during the first year of college: career exploration activities, courses in common, college transition courses, first-year seminars, racial/cultural awareness workshops, Greek affiliation, university honors program, intramural sports, living-learning residences, on-campus lectures on political or social issues, out-of-class research projects with a faculty member, campus leadership positions, and leadership training experiences.

Exposure to Effective Classroom Instruction. Overall exposure to effective classroom instruction was defined operationally as exposure to

NEW DIRECTIONS FOR TEACHING AND LEARNING • DOI: 10.1002/tl

Exhibit 4.1. Constituent Items for the Instructional Organization and Clarity Scale

Scale stem: Below are statements about teacher skill/clarity as well as preparation and organization in teaching. For the most part, taking into consideration all of the teachers with whom you've interacted at [university name], how often have you experienced each? Response options: 5 = "very often"; 4 = "often"; 3 = "sometimes"; 2 = "rarely"; 1 = "never."

The scale score was computed as the average score for each item (mean = 3.789, standard deviation = .529).

Presentation of material is well organized.
Teachers are well prepared for class.
Class time is used effectively.
Course goals and requirements are clearly explained.
Teachers have good command of what they are teaching.
Teachers give clear explanations.
Teachers make good use of examples and illustrations to explain difficult points.
Teachers effectively review and summarize the material.
Teachers interpret abstract ideas and theories clearly.
Teachers give assignments that help in learning the course material.

Note: Alpha reliability = .91.

organized and clear instruction. Information on student perceptions of exposure to organized and clear instruction was collected by means of a ten-item scale in the Web-based survey. The item on the survey presented students with the following stem: "Below are statements about teacher skill/clarity as well as preparation and organization in teaching. For the most part, taking into consideration all of the teachers with whom you've interacted with at [university name], how often have you experienced each?"

Students were presented with the same ten items of vetted reliability and validity used in studies described above (Braxton, Bray, and Berger, 2000; Bray, Pascarella, and Pierson, 2004; Edison, Doyle, and Pascarella, 1998; Pascarella and others, 1996; Whitt and others, 2003). All of the specific items are shown in Exhibit 4.1. The response options were: 5 = Very Often, 4 = Often, 3 = Sometimes, 2 = Rarely, and 1 = Never. Because prior research has shown that the separate five-item scales organization/preparation and skill/clarity are so highly collinear (r = .73; see Bray, Pascarella, and Pierson, 2004), we combined the ten items into a single scale: instructional organization and clarity. For the study sample, the internal consistency (alpha) reliability for this scale was .91—clearly supporting the contention that the ten items are in all likelihood measuring a single underlying instructional trait.

Cumulative College Grades. "Cumulative college grades" was defined operationally as a student's cumulative grade point average across the first two semesters of college. Data on this variable were obtained from the office of the university registrar.

Educational Satisfaction. The Web-based survey offered respondents a single item on which they could indicate their satisfaction with the education being received. The specific item was: "Overall, how satisfied are you with the education you are receiving at [institutional name]? The response options were 5 = Very Satisfied, 4 = Satisfied, 3 = Neither Satisfied nor Dissatisfied, 2 = Dissatisfied, and 1 = Very Dissatisfied. Because this variable was so positively skewed, we recoded it into two dummy variables, Very Satisfied and Satisfied, with the comparison group being Neither Satisfied nor Dissatisfied, Dissatisfied, or Very Dissatisfied.

Educational Degree Plans. This was a single item on the Web-based survey that asked students to indicate the highest academic degree they intended to earn in their lifetime. The response options were bachelor's degree, master's degree, law (J.D.), and doctorate (Ph.D., Ed.D., M.D.). The item was coded any graduate degree = 1 and bachelor's degree = 0.

Persistence into the Second Year of College. The persistence variable was defined operationally as whether a student reenrolled for the second year of postsecondary education at the study institution. It was coded 1 = reenrolled, and 0 = did not reenroll and was obtained from official records held by the university office of the registrar. Of the 1,353 students in the sample, 1,228 students (90.8 percent) reenrolled for the second year of college and 125 (9.2 percent) did not.

Data Analyses. The first step in the data analyses was to estimate the total effect of overall exposure to organized and clear instruction during the first year of college on persistence into the second year of college. For this, we used reduced form regression specifications (Alwin and Hauser, 1975) and, because the dependent variable was binomial (1 = reenrolled, 0 = did not reenroll) rather than continuous, logistic rather than linear regression. Persistence was regressed on the measure of overall exposure to organized and clear instruction and all background characteristics, ACT composite score, and other college experiences (see Figure 4.1). The second step in the analyses sought to determine the direct and indirect (or mediated) effects of organized and clear instruction on persistence. For this analysis, we added cumulative first-year college grades, satisfaction with the education being received, and educational degree plans to the reduced-form (total effects) specification described above (see Figure 4.2). According to our conceptual model, we expected that college grades, educational satisfaction, and degree plans would have a positive influence on persistence and that the positive total effect of organized and clear instruction on persistence would be reduced to nonsignificance. Thus, the enhancement of grades, satisfaction, and degree plans would mediate (or account for) the positive impact of organized and clear instruction on persistence.

To isolate which, if any, of the three mediating variables transmitted most of the indirect effect of exposure to organized and clear instruction on second-year persistence, we tested several models. Grades, satisfaction, and degree plans were added to the total effects equation in different combinations to determine if the addition of any single mediating variable reduced the estimated effect of organized and clear instruction to nonsignificance. Because of the large sample size ($N = 1,353$), we used .01 as the critical level of statistical significance in all analyses.

Results of the Study

The estimated total and direct effects of overall exposure to organized and clear instruction on persistence into the second year of college are summarized in Table 4.1. Columns 1 and 2 in Table 4.1 show the results of the total effect estimate. As the table indicates, in the presence of statistical controls for student background characteristics, ACT composite score, and an extensive array of other first-year college experiences (see note a in Table 4.1), overall exposure to organized and clear instruction significantly ($p < .001$) increased the probability of a student reenrolling for the second year of postsecondary education at the study institution. The odds ratio in column 2 indicates that net of the influence of all other variables in the total effect equation, a one-point increase on the instructional organization and clarity scale increased the odds of reenrolling from even (1.00/1.00) to 1.78/1.00. This can be thought of as a 78 percent improvement in the odds of reenrolling. Since the aggregate sample standard deviation of the organized and clear instruction scale was .529 (recall that an individual's scale score was the average score on each item), this means that an increase of one standard deviation on the scale increases the net odds of reenrolling from even (1.00/1.00) to 1.41/1.00 (the increase in odds, or .78 × .529). This can be interpreted as a 41 percent increase in the odds of reenrolling.

Columns 3 and 4 in Table 4.1 (direct effect, model I) summarize the estimated direct causal effect of overall exposure to organized and clear instruction on persistence when cumulative first-year grades and graduate degree plans were added to the total effect equation (summarized in columns 1 and 2). It is not surprising that first-year grades had a strong and statistically significant positive effect on the probability of second-year enrollment, although graduate degree plans did not. What is more important is that even with additional controls made for academic achievement and degree plans, exposure to organized and clear instruction continued to exert a significant, positive influence on the likelihood of reenrolling at the institution for the second year of college. Indeed, the magnitude of the net effect of organized and clear instruction on persistence was reduced only a trivial amount from the total effect equation (regression coefficient reduced from .578 to .544, odds ratio reduced from 1.78 to 1.72) and remained statistically significant at $p < .005$. With additional controls for grades and degree plans, an increase of one standard deviation in exposure to organized and clear instruction produced an increase in the odds of reenrolling from even (1.00/1.00) to 1.38/1.00. Thus, somewhat contrary to expectations, our findings suggest that overall exposure to organized and clear instruc-

Table 4.1. Estimated Total and Direct Effects of Exposure to Organized and Clear Instruction on Persistence into the Second Year of College

Variable	Total Effect[a]		Direct Effect[a] Model I		Direct Effect[a] Model II	
	(1) Regression Coefficient (Standard Error)	(2) Odds Ratio	(3) Regression Coefficient (Standard Error)	(4) Odds Ratio	(5) Regression Coefficient (Standard Error)	(6) Odds Ratio
Instructional organization and clarity scale	.578** (.174)	1.783	.544* (.181)	1.724	.179 (.200)	1.196
Cumulative first-year grade point average			1.417** (.189)	4.132	1.394** (.194)	4.031
Graduate degree plans			.284 (.241)	1.328	.215 (.333)	1.240
Educational satisfaction Very satisfied[b]					1.266** (.333)	3.546
Satisfied[b]					−.091 (.292)	.913

[a]Logistic regression equations also include controls for ACT composite score; sex; race; father's degree attainment; mother's degree attainment; whether one was receiving financial aid; hours per week of on-campus work; hours per week of off-campus work; first-year place of residence (fraternity/ sorority house, off campus within three miles of campus, and off campus farther than three miles from campus versus campus housing); intended major (arts and humanities, education, engineering, journalism/communications, natural sciences, social sciences, nursing, and other versus business); reported binge drinking during a typical two-week period (once, twice, three to five times, six or more times versus never); and participation in thirteen other experiences or programs during the first year of college (career exploration, courses in common, college transition courses, first-year seminars, racial/cultural awareness workshops, Greek affiliation, university honors program, intramural sports, living-learning residences, on-campus lectures on political or social issues, out-of-class research projects with a faculty member, held a campus leadership position, and leadership training experiences). All results reported are based on the weighted sample adjusted to the unweighted sample size to obtain correct standard errors.

[b]Comparison group is students who indicated "neither satisfied nor dissatisfied," "dissatisfied," or "very dissatisfied."

*$p < .005$. **$p < .001$.

tion has a significant, positive net effect on persistence that is independent not only of student background characteristics, ACT scores, and an extensive array of other college experiences, but also of cumulative first-year college grades and graduate degree plans.

It was only when the dummy variables representing satisfaction with the education one was receiving were added to the equation (columns 5 and 6, direct effect, model II) that the total effect of organized and clear instruction on persistence was dramatically reduced (from .578 to .179) and became

NEW DIRECTIONS FOR TEACHING AND LEARNING • DOI: 10.1002/tl

statistically nonsignificant. Such a finding indicates that of the estimated indirect effect of organized and clear instruction on persistence (.578 − .179, or .399, see Table 4.1, columns 1 and 5), about 91 percent (.544 − .179, or .365, see Table 4.1, columns 3 and 5) was mediated through increased satisfaction with the education one was receiving at the study institution.

We tested the statistical significance of the indirect effect of exposure to organized and clear instruction through satisfaction using Sobel's procedure for the significance of mediated effects (Preacher and Leonardelli, 2001). This test indicated that a statistically significant ($p < .01$) and positive indirect effect of organized and clear instruction on persistence was mediated through the dummy variable that compared students who were "very satisfied" with the education they were receiving to a group composed of those who indicated that they were "neither satisfied nor dissatisfied," "unsatisfied," or "very dissatisfied." In short, net of other factors, students exposed to organized and clear instruction were more likely to report being "very satisfied" with the education they were receiving at the institution. In turn, being "very satisfied" with one's educational experience during the first year of college improved the likelihood of reenrolling at the institution for the second year of college significantly.

Finally, we conducted a series of analyses to determine if the direct effects of exposure to organized and clear instruction on persistence differed significantly in magnitude for men versus women, white students versus students of color, and students with different ACT scores. These analyses were all nonsignificant at the .01 level. There was a marginally significant ($p < .05$) trend for the positive effects of organized and clear instruction to be somewhat more pronounced for women than for men. However, there was no evidence to suggest that the effects of exposure to organized and clear instruction on persistence differed in more than chance ways for white students versus students of color or for students with different ACT scores.

Summary and Conclusions

In this chapter, we have reviewed a small but growing body of evidence suggesting that exposure to effective classroom instruction in college has implications beyond the facilitation of knowledge acquisition in a specific course. Exposure to overall organized and clear instruction across the classes one takes in college appears to enhance not only the development of general cognitive skills not directly linked to a specific course but also the intention to reenroll at a specific postsecondary institution. Extending the work of Braxton, Bray, and Berger (2000), we described a study suggesting that overall exposure to organized and clear instruction during the first year of postsecondary education at a large, public research university significantly increased the probability of reenrollment at that institution for the second year of college.

The study employed a ten-item scale of demonstrated reliability and validity that measured a student's reported overall exposure to organized and clear instruction across all of their first-year courses and teachers. Controlling for background characteristics, ACT score, and an extensive array of other first-year experiences and involvements, overall exposure to organized and clear instruction had a significant ($p < .001$) positive total effect on reenrolling for the second year of college. An increase of one standard deviation on the instructional organization and clarity scale was associated with a net increase in the odds of reenrolling from even (1.00/1.00) to 1.41/1.00. Exposure to organized and clear instruction continued to have a significant ($p < .005$) net impact on reenrollment decisions even after taking into account the additional influence of cumulative first-year college grades and graduate degree plans. With these two variables added to the total effect equation, an increase of one standard deviation on the instructional organization and clarity scale was still linked with a net increase in the odds of reenrolling from even (1.00/1.00) to 1.38/1.00. Moreover, although there was marginally significant evidence to suggest that the unmediated positive effects of organized and clear instruction on persistence were somewhat more pronounced for women than men, we uncovered no evidence to suggest that such effects differed in magnitude for white students versus students of color or for students with different levels of pre-college academic preparation.

Our analyses suggest that most of the causal influence of overall exposure to organized and clear instruction on reenrollment decisions is indirect, being mediated (or accounted for) by level of satisfaction with the first-year education one is receiving. Net of other influences, overall exposure to organized and clear instruction during the first year of college increases the likelihood that a student will be "very satisfied" with the undergraduate education he or she is receiving. In turn, this satisfaction has a net positive influence on the likelihood one will reenroll for the second year of undergraduate education at an institution.

Although our findings are somewhat limited in generalizability by the single-institution sample, they might have reasonably clear implications for policy or practice. A substantial body of evidence has indicated that the frequency and quality of faculty members' nonclassroom interactions with students play a significant role in students' decisions to persist at a particular college or university (Pascarella and Terenzini, 1991, 2005). Our findings underscore the salience of faculty behaviors in student persistence decisions by suggesting that it is not just their nonclassroom interactions with students that count, but also their actual classroom instructional behaviors. Exposure to instructional behaviors that enhance learning (organization and clarity) might also increase the probability of a student's persistence at an institution by increasing his or her sense of overall satisfaction with the education being received. Perhaps of equal, if not greater, importance to policymakers is the implication that delivering organized and clear class-room instruction might not be merely a function of an individual faculty member's innate skills or propensities. Rather, as Weimer and Lenze (1997) suggested, faculty members can learn many of the constituent skills and behaviors required to implement organized and clear instruction in their courses. A variety of methods and mechanisms has been employed on many campuses to provide faculty members with assistance in developing and improving teaching effectiveness. This study provides evidence of the poten-tial impact of such efforts on student success as measured by retention and could argue for their expansion. Policies requiring faculty to engage in development activities to improve effectiveness are unlikely at most colleges and universities, but providing faculty, administrators, and students with evidence that good teaching matters for student persistence could help cre-ate a climate in which activities to improve teaching are a taken-for-granted aspect of faculty work. From this perspective, our findings lend support to the potential institutional benefits derived from the investment of resources in programs designed to enhance teaching effectiveness, particularly to the extent that these programs help faculty hone sound pedagogical skills such as instructional organization and clarity.

References

Aleamoni, L. M. "Student Rating Myths Versus Research Facts from 1924 to 1998." *Journal of Personnel Evaluation in Education*, 1999, *13*, 153–166.

Alwin, D. F., and Hauser, R. M. "The Decomposition of Effects in Path Analysis." *American Sociological Review*, 1975, *40*, 37–47.

Braskamp, L. A., and Ory, J. C. *Assessing Faculty Work: Enhancing Individual and Institutional Performance.* San Francisco: Jossey-Bass, 1994.

Braxton, J. M., Bray, N. J., and Berger, J. B. "Faculty Teaching Skills and Their Influences on the College Student Departure Process." *Journal of College Student Development*, 2000, *41*, 215–227.

Braxton, J. M., Hirschy, A., and McClendon, S. A. *Understanding and Reducing College Student Departure.* ASHE-ERIC Higher Education Report, vol. 30, no. 3. San Francisco: Jossey-Bass, 2004.

Braxton, J. M., and McClendon, S. A. "The Fostering of Social Integration and Reten-tion Through Institutional Practice." *Journal of College Student Retention*, 2001–2002, *3*, 57–71.

Braxton, J. M., Milem, J. F., and Sullivan, A. S. "The Influence of Active Learning on the College Student Departure Process: Toward a Revision of Tinto's Theory." *Journal of Higher Education*, 2000, *71*, 569–590.

Braxton, J. M., and Mundy, M. E. "Powerful Institutional Levers to Reduce College Stu-dent Departure." *Journal of College Student Retention*, 2001–2002, *3*, 91–118.

Bray, G., Pascarella, E. T., and Pierson, C. T. "Postsecondary Education and Some Dimensions of Literacy Development: An Exploration of Longitudinal Evidence." *Reading Research Quarterly*, 2004, *39*, 306–330.

Cashin, W. "Student Ratings of Teaching: Their Uses and Misuses." Unpublished man-uscript, Kansas State University, 1999.

Cohen, P. A. "Student Ratings of Instruction and Student Achievement: A Meta-Analysis of Multisection Validity Studies." *Review of Educational Research*, 1981, *51*, 281–309.

d'Apollonia, S., and Abrami, P. C. "Navigating Student Ratings of Instruction." *American Psychologist,* 1997, *52,* 1198–1208.

Edison, M., Doyle, S., and Pascarella, E. "Dimensions of Teaching Effectiveness and Their Impact on Student Cognitive Development." Paper presented at the meeting of the Association for the Study of Higher Education, Miami, Fla., Nov. 1998.

Feldman, K. A. "The Association Between Student Ratings of Specific Instructional Dimensions and Student Achievement: Refining and Extending the Synthesis of Data from Multisection Validity Studies." *Research in Higher Education,* 1989, *30,* 583–645.

Feldman, K. "Identifying Exemplary Teaching: Evidence from Course and Teacher Evaluations." Paper commissioned by the National Center on Postsecondary Teaching, Learning, and Assessment, State University of New York at Stony Brook, 1994.

Feldman, K. A. "Identifying Exemplary Teachers and Teaching: Evidence from Student Ratings." In R. Perry and J. Smart (eds.), *Effective Teaching in Higher Education: Research and Practice.* Edison, N.J.: Agathon Press, 1997.

Goodman, K., and Pascarella, E. "First-Year Seminars Increase Persistence and Retention: A Summary of the Evidence from *How College Affects Students." Peer Review: Journal of the Association of American Colleges and Universities,* 2006, *8*(3), 26–28.

Greenwald, A. A. "Validity Concerns and Usefulness of Student Ratings of Instruction." *American Psychologist,* 1997, *52,* 1182–1186.

Greenwald, A. A., and Gillmore, G. M. "Grading Leniency Is a Removable Contaminant of Student Ratings." *American Psychologist,* 1997, *52,* 1209–1217.

Hines, C. V., Cruickshank, D. R., and Kennedy, J. J. "Teacher Clarity and Its Relationship to Student Achievement and Satisfaction." *American Educational Research Journal,* 1985, *22,* 87–99.

Krautmann, A. C., and Sander, W. "Grades and Student Evaluations of Teachers." *Economics of Education Review,* 1999, *18,* 59–63.

Marsh, H., and Dunkin, M. "Students' Evaluations of University Teaching: A Multidimensional Perspective." In R. Perry and J. Smart (eds.), *Effective Teaching in Higher Education: Research and Practice.* New York: Agathon, 1997.

McKeachie, W. J. "Student Ratings: The Validity of Use." *American Psychologist,* 1997, *52,* 1218–1225.

Murray, H. G., Jelley, R. B., and Renaud, R. D. "Longitudinal Trends in Student Instructional Ratings: Does Evaluation of Teaching Lead to Improvement of Teaching?" Paper read at American Educational Research Association, New York, Apr. 1996.

Nora, A., Cabrera, A., Hagedorn, L., and Pascarella, E. "Differential Impacts of Academic and Social Experiences on College-Related Behavioral Outcomes Across Different Ethnic and Gender Groups at Four-Year Institutions." *Research in Higher Education,* 1996, *37,* 427–451.

Pascarella, E. T. "How College Affects Students: Ten Directions for Future Research." *Journal of College Student Development,* 2006, *47,* 508–520.

Pascarella, E., and others. "Effects of Teacher Organization/Preparation and Teacher Skill/Clarity on General Cognitive Skills in College." *Journal of College Student Development,* 1996, *37,* 7–19.

Pascarella, E. T., and Terenzini, P. T. *How College Affects Students: Findings and Insights from Twenty Years of Research.* San Francisco: Jossey-Bass, 1991.

Pascarella, E. T., and Terenzini, P. T. *How College Affects Students,* Vol. 2: *A Third Decade of Research.* San Francisco: Jossey-Bass, 2005.

Pascarella, E. T., Wolniak, G. C., Pierson, C. T., and Flowers, L. A. "The Role of Race in the Development of Plans for a Graduate Degree." *Review of Higher Education,* 2004, *27,* 299–320.

Preacher, K. J., and Leonardelli, G. J. "Calculation for the Sobel Test: An Interactive Calculation Tool for Mediation Tests." 2001. Retrieved June 20, 2007, from www.unc.edu/~preacher/sobel/sobel.htm.

Schonwetter, D., Menec, V., and Perry, R. "An Empirical Comparison of Two Effective College Teaching Behaviors: Expressiveness and Organization." Paper presented at the annual meeting of the American Educational Research Association, San Francisco, Apr. 1995.

Schonwetter, D., Perry, R. P., and Struthers, C. W. "Students' Perceptions of Control and Success in the College Classroom: Affects and Achievement in Different Instructional Conditions." *Journal of Experimental Education*, 1994, *61*, 227–246.

Tinto, V. "Dropout from Higher Education: A Theoretical Synthesis of Recent Research." *Review of Educational Research*, 1975, *45*, 89–125.

Tinto, V. *Leaving College: Rethinking the Causes and Cures of Student Attrition.* (2nd ed.) Chicago: University of Chicago Press, 1993.

Tinto, V. "Colleges as Communities: Exploring the Educational Character of Student Persistence." *Journal of Higher Education*, 1997, *68*, 599–623.

Tinto, V. "Research and Practice of Student Retention: What Next?" *Journal of College Student Retention*, 2006–2007, *8*, 1–19.

Wachtel, H. J. "Student Evaluation of College Teaching Effectiveness: A Brief Review." *Assessment and Evaluation in Higher Education*, 1998, *23*, 191–211.

Weimer, M., and Lenze, L. "Instructional Interventions: Review of the Literature on Efforts to Improve Instruction." In R. Perry and J. Smart (eds.), *Effective Teaching in Higher Education: Research and Practice.* New York: Agathon Press, 1997.

Whitt, E. J., and others. "Differences Between Women and Men in Objectively Measured Outcomes, and the Factors That Influence Those Outcomes, in the First Three Years of College." *Journal of College Student Development*, 2003, *44*, 587–610.

Wood, A., and Murray, H. "Effects of Teacher Enthusiasm on Student Attention, Motivation, and Memory Encoding." Paper presented at the annual meeting of the American Educational Research Association, Montreal, Canada, Apr. 1999.

ERNEST T. PASCARELLA *is the Petersen Professor of Higher Education at the University of Iowa.*

TRICIA A. SEIFERT *is a postdoctoral scholar at the University of Iowa.*

ELIZABETH J. WHITT *is professor of student affairs and higher education at the University of Iowa.*

*The primary goal of this study was to examine the impact
of active learning on a student's level of overall social
integration and perception of his or her institution's
commitment to student welfare.*

The Role of Active Learning in College Student Persistence

*John M. Braxton, Willis A. Jones, Amy S. Hirschy, and
Harold V. Hartley III*

Active learning, which entails any class activity that "involves students doing
things and thinking about the things that they are doing" (Bonwell and
Eison, 1991, p. 2), stands as an important pedagogical practice. Discussion,
the types of questions faculty ask students in class, role playing, cooperative
learning, debates, and the types of questions faculty ask on examinations represent forms of active learning (Braxton, Milem, and Sullivan, 2000).

The importance of active learning stems from the contribution it makes
to fostering undergraduate college student success (Braxton, forthcoming).
Student knowledge and understanding of course content benefit from the
use of active learning by college and university faculty members (Anderson
and Adams, 1992; Chickering and Gamson, 1987; Johnson, Johnson, and
Smith, 1991; McKeachie, Pintrich, Yi-Guang, and Smith, 1986). Chickering
and Gamson (1987) identify active learning as one of their seven principles
of good practice for undergraduate education. These seven principles rest
on a base of empirical research that indicates that faculty adherence to the
principles has a positive impact on student learning (Sorcinelli, 1991).

In addition to increasing student course learning, faculty use of active
learning practices directly and indirectly affects college student departure

---

Contact the authors to receive a copy of the full logistic regression model used in this
chapter.

NEW DIRECTIONS FOR TEACHING AND LEARNING, no. 115, Fall 2008   © Wiley Periodicals, Inc.
Published online in Wiley InterScience (www.interscience.wiley.com) • DOI: 10.1002/tl.326

decisions (Braxton, Milem, and Sullivan, 2000). Class discussions, a form of active learning, wield a positive influence on social integration, subsequent commitment to the institution, and intent to return to the focal university in the subsequent fall semester (Braxton, Milem and Sullivan, 2000). Intent to return was used as proxy indicator of student departure, a measure based on a strong positive relationship between intent to return and actual student persistence (Bean, 1980, 1983; Pascarella, Duby, and Iverson, 1983; Voorhees, 1987; Cabrera, Casteneda, Nora, and Hengstler, 1992). Social integration, subsequent institutional commitment, and persistence correspond to propositions of Tinto's interactionalist theory of college student departure that receive strong empirical backing in residential institutions (Braxton, Sullivan, and Johnson, 1997).

Although Braxton, Milem, and Sullivan (2000) found a positive link between active learning in the form of class discussions and subsequent institutional commitment and the intent to return, their primary focus centered on the role of active learning in fostering the social integration of students. The research reported in this chapter also focuses on the influence of active learning on the level of social integration that students experience. Put differently, this research endeavors to replicate and extend the work of Braxton, Milem, and Sullivan (2000).

Three factors provide a strong rationale for the replication and extension of this research. The importance of replication of research stands as one of these factors. Through replication, reliable knowledge obtains (Braxton and Lee, 2005). Another basis pertains to the use of an actual measure of student persistence in this research rather than intent to return, as used by Braxton, Milem, and Sullivan (2000). Braxton, Milem, and Johnson acknowledge the use of intent to return rather than an actual measure of persistence as a limitation to their research. The third factor entails the institutional setting of Braxton, Milem, and Sullivan's research. A highly selective private research university provided the setting for their research. Braxton, Milem, and Sullivan also recognize the institutional setting for their research as a limitation; they suggest that the findings of their study might not be generalizable to other types of colleges and universities. In particular, the positive influence of active learning on social integration might not obtain in other types of colleges and universities.

Thus, the research reported in this chapter centers on the influence of faculty use of active learning practices on social integration, uses an actual measure of student persistence, and uses a sample of students enrolled in eight religiously affiliated, residential, private colleges and universities. This study also focuses on the influence of active learning on shaping student perceptions of the commitment of their college or university to the welfare of its students. Braxton, Hirschy, and McClendon (2004) posit commitment of the institution to the welfare of its students as an antecedent of social integration.

Theoretical Framework

Student entry characteristics shape students' initial level of commitment to their college or university. Such entry characteristics include family background (such as parental educational level and parental income), individual attributes (gender, racial/ethnic membership), and precollege schooling experiences (for example, high school record of academic achievement) (Tinto, 1975). The initial level of institutional commitment affects the student's perceptions of the commitment of their college or university to the welfare of its students (Braxton, Hirschy, and McClendon, 2004). The more a student perceives that his or her college or university is committed to the welfare of its students, the greater the student's level of social integration (Braxton, Hirschy, and McClendon, 2004). A college or university displays a commitment to the welfare of its students by communicating an abiding concern for its students' growth and development. The high value an institution places on students as individuals and in groups also indexes its commitment to the welfare of these students. A college or university also exhibits a commitment to the welfare of its students by treating students equitably and with respect as individuals (Braxton, Hirschy, and McClendon, 2004). Social integration results when students perceive that their college or university demonstrates a strong commitment to their welfare and become motivated to establish membership in the social communities of their college or university (Braxton, Milem, and Sullivan, 2000; Milem and Berger, 1997).

Social integration pertains to the extent of congruency between the individual student and the social system of a college or university. As such, it indexes the student's perception of his or her degree of congruence with the attitudes, values, beliefs, and norms of the social communities of a college or university, as well as his or her degree of social affiliation. Social integration also occurs at the level of the college or university and its subculture (Tinto, 1975).

Social integration exerts an influence on the student's subsequent level of commitment to the college or university. The greater the student's level of social integration, the greater is his or her degree of subsequent commitment to the college or university. The student's initial level of commitment to the college or university also shapes his or her degree of subsequent commitment to their institution. The greater the student's subsequent commitment to the college or university, the greater his or her likelihood of persistence (Tinto, 1975).

An abiding concern for the growth and development of its students stands as a key aspect of the notion of the commitment of the institution to the welfare of its students (Braxton, Hirschy, and McClendon, 2004). Because active learning enhances student knowledge and understanding of the content of academic courses (Anderson and Adams, 1992; Chickering and Gamson, 1987; Johnson, Johnson, and Smith, 1991; McKeachie, Pintrich, Yi-Guang, and Smith, 1986), faculty members who use this pedagogical practice may contribute to their institution's abiding concern for the growth and development of its students. These formulations suggest the following hypothesis: the more frequently students perceive that faculty members use active learning practices in their courses, the more that students perceive that their college or university is committed to its students' welfare.

Faculty use of active learning practices also influences the student's level of social integration. To elaborate, students who experience active learning in their courses perceive themselves as gaining knowledge and understanding from their courses and view their course work as personally rewarding (Braxton, Milem, and Sullivan, 2000). Such perceptions motivate students to devote the psychological energy needed to establish membership in the social communities of their institution (Braxton, Milem, and Sullivan, 2000; Milem and Berger, 1997).

Moreover, increases in the learning of course content due to faculty use of active learning practices may also give students more discretionary time to engage in the life of the social communities of their college or university (Braxton, Milem, and Sullivan, 2000). Active learning activities encourage interaction among students in the classroom, and these classroom interactions may lead to the development of friendships that extend beyond the classroom. Thus, the more frequently students perceive that faculty members use active learning practices in their courses, the greater is their degree of social integration.

To sum up, this theoretical framework yields the following directional hypotheses:

HYPOTHESIS 1. *The more frequently students perceive that faculty members use active learning practices in their courses, the more that students perceive that their college or university is committed to the welfare of its students.*
HYPOTHESIS 2. *The more frequently students perceive that faculty members use active learning practices in their courses, the greater is their degree of social integration.*
HYPOTHESIS 3. *The greater a student's degree of social integration, the greater is that student's level of subsequent commitment to the college or university.*
HYPOTHESIS 4. *The greater a student's level of subsequent commitment to the college or university, the greater is his or her likelihood of persistence in that college or university.*

Methods

This study uses a longitudinal panel design of 408 first-time, full-time, first-year students in eight residential and religiously affiliated colleges and universities to test the four hypotheses. Students were randomly selected at each institution participating in a study of undergraduate experiences in the first year of college. The data collection for this study consisted of the administration of *The Fall Collegiate Experiences Survey* in fall 2002, the administration of *The Spring Collegiate Experiences Survey* in spring 2003, and the fall 2003 enrollment records of the eight participating colleges and universities. The two surveys were distributed to random samples of first-year students at each institution. The longitudinal panel was constructed using the responses to the two surveys and the fall 2003 institutional enrollment records with student cases matched by their identification number across the three data collection points.

The sample of 408 students represents an aggregate response rate of 28.4 percent across the eight participating colleges and universities. Nearly 60 percent of the students were female (59.8 percent, $n = 244$), and 12.8 percent were minority ($n = 52$). Of the eight institutions from which the sample was drawn, one is a master's I, four are baccalaureate-general, and three are baccalaureate–liberal arts. Due to the relatively low response rate in this study, cases from two of the eight institutions were weighted to ensure some degree of representativeness to their respective campus populations on gender and race.

From these two surveys, seven sets of variables that operationalize key concepts from the theoretical framework described above were derived:

1. Student entry characteristics (gender, race/ethnicity, parental education level, parental income, and average grades earned in high school)
2. Initial institutional commitment
3. Faculty use of active learning practices
4. Commitment of the institution to student welfare
5. Social integration
6. Subsequent institutional commitment
7. Student persistence

Table 5.1 displays the operational definitions of the variables that make up these seven sets of variables. In their research, Braxton, Milem, and Sullivan (2000) used four composite variables to measure active learning: class discussion, higher-order thinking activities, examination questions limited to knowledge of facts, and group work. In contrast, this study measures faculty use of active learning practices with a composite variable that has one item tapping classroom discussions and four items that plumb classroom higher-order thinking activities. A narrower perspective on active learning was used in this study because of the unavailability of items included on the two surveys used in this piece of research. Table 5.1 exhibits the five survey items used in the research to measure faculty use of active learning practices. These five items coincide with those of Bonwell and Eison's definition of active learning (1991) as any classroom activity that "involves students in doing things and thinking about the things they are doing" (p. 2).

NEW DIRECTIONS FOR TEACHING AND LEARNING • DOI: 10.1002/tl

Table 5.1. Definition of Dependent and Independent Variables

Variable	Definition
Female	Student gender (male = 0; female = 1)
Minority	Student racial/ethnic identity in comparison to the student population of institution attended (majority = 0; minority = 1)
High School Grades	Self-reported high school cumulative grade point average (C1 = 1; A or A+ = 8)
Parental Income	Student-reported estimated parental income (less than $6,000 = 1; $200,000 or more = 14)
Parental Education Level	Level of parental educational attainment (grammar school or less for both parents = 2; graduate work for both parents = 16). Composite variable is sum of two items: father's level of educational attainment and mother's level
Initial Institutional Commitment	Ranking of student's college choice (fourth choice or more = 1; first choice = 4)
Active Learning	Composite of five items that measure active learning as any classroom activity that "involves students in doing things and thinking about the things they are doing." These five items focus on the frequency of instructors' engaging in classroom discussion or debate of course ideas and concepts, ask me to point out any fallacies in basic ideas, principles, or points of view presented in the course, ask me to argue for or against a particular point of view, require me to argue for or against a particular point of view and defend my argument in a course paper or research project, and require me to propose a plan for a research project or experiment for a course paper. 1 = never, 4 = very often. Cronbach's alpha = .75.
Institutional Commitment to the Welfare of Students	Composite of ten items measuring student perceptions that the institution is committed to the welfare of students: most student services staff (for example, dean of students office, student activities, housing) are genuinely interested in students, most other college/university staff (for example, registrar, student accounts, financial aid) are genuinely interested in students, most of the campus religious leaders (for example, chaplain, priest, rabbi) are genuinely interested in students, have experienced negative interactions with faculty members (reverse scored), have experienced negative interactions with student services staff (reverse scored), have experienced negative interactions with other college/university staff (reverse scored), faculty members treat students with respect, student services staff treat students with respect, other college/university staff treat students with respect, know where to go if need more information about a policy. Strongly disagree = 1; strongly agree = 4. Cronbach's alpha = .86.
Social Integration	Composite of seven items measuring the degree of a student's integration into campus social system: interpersonal relationships with other students have had influence on intellectual growth; developed close personal relationships with peers; peer relationships have had influence on personal growth, values, and

(continued)

Table 5.1. (continued)

Variable	Definition
	attitudes; difficulty making friends (reverse scored); few peers would listen to personal problems (reverse scored); peer friendships have been satisfying; student's attitudes and values differ from peers' (reverse scored). Strongly disagree = 1; strongly agree = 4. Cronbach's alpha = .79
Subsequent Institutional Commitment	Composite of two items measuring degree of subsequent commitment to college of enrollment: not important to graduate from this college (reverse scored), made the right decision in choosing to attend this college. Strongly disagree = 1; strongly agree = 4.
Persistence	Student's decision to reenroll at institution for fall: Data source for enrollment status provided by seven institutions (not enrolled = 0; enrolled = 1); source of data for one institution was student response to intent-to-reenroll item on spring survey (recoded strongly disagree or disagree = 0; agree or strongly agree = 1)

Statistical Design

Four hierarchical linear regression analyses were used to test this study's four hypotheses. In addition to controlling for student entry characteristics and the student's initial level of institutional commitment, each of these regression analyses also controlled for the possible unique effects of the three Carnegie Classification institutional types (Baccalaureate Colleges–General, Baccalaureate Colleges–Liberal Arts, Master's Colleges and Universities I) represented in this study. To control for the unique effects of these three institution types, dummy variables were constructed (1 = focal institution type, 0 = other institution types). These dummy variables were entered into four regression analyses prior to student entry characteristics and initial level of institutional commitment. The .05 level of statistical significance was used to identify statistically significant relationships.

The fourth hypothesis of this study was also tested using logistical regression. Logistical regression was used because of the dichotomous and highly skewed distribution of the measure of student persistence. Logistical regression was used to verify the results of the fourth hierarchical linear regression equation estimated.

Findings

Table 5.2 displays the results of the regression analysis testing hypothesis 1 and hypothesis 2 of this study. Model I uses a student's perception of his or her institution's commitment to student welfare as the dependent variable,

Table 5.2. OLS Estimates of the Impact of Active Learning on Student Perception of Institutional Commitment to Students and Overall Student Integration

	Model I	Model II
Active Learning	0.136***	−0.024
	(0.039)	(0.035)
Gender	0.092	0.060
	(0.048)	(0.043)
Minority	−0.018	−0.104
	(0.070)	(0.062)
Parent Income	0.022**	0.007
	(0.007)	(0.007)
Parent Education	0.004	0.013
	(0.009)	(0.007)
High School Grades	0.009	−0.002
	(0.014)	(0.012)
Initial Institutional Commitment	0.014	0.054*
	(0.029)	(0.025)
Institutional commitment to student welfare	—	0.449***
	—	(0.044)
Constant	2.207***	1.271***
Observations	407	407
R-squared	0.109	0.299

Note: Standard errors in parentheses

*Significant at .05 level. **Significant at .01 level. ***Significant at .001 level.

and model II uses a student's degree of social integration as the dependent variable. The results indicate that after controlling for a student's demographic information and initial institutional commitment, student perceptions of faculty use of active learning practices have a positive and statistically significant ($\beta = .136$, $p = .001$) impact on how students perceive their institution's commitment to the welfare of students. The relationship between active learning and a student's degree of overall social integration, however, failed to provide a statistically reliable coefficient ($\beta = −0.024$, $p = .493$). However, model II indicates that student perceptions of the extent to which their college or university displays a commitment to the welfare of its students exert a positive direct influence on social integration ($\beta = .449$, $p = .001$).

Tables 5.3 and 5.4 display the findings of the regression analysis testing hypothesis 3 and 4 of this study. Table 5.3 supports the findings of Braxton, Sullivan, and Johnson (1997) and Braxton, Milem, and Sullivan (2000) that social integration is positively and significantly related to a student's subsequent institutional commitment. This table also indicates that a student's level of subsequent institutional commitment is positively related to a student's perception of the institution's commitment to students ($\beta = .511$, $p = .000$), a student's high school grades ($\beta = .04$, $p = .027$), and a student's

**Table 5.3. OLS Estimates of the Impact of Social
Integration on Subsequent Institutional Commitment**

Social Integration	0.280***
	(0.075)
Institutional Commitment to Student Welfare	0.511***
	(0.074)
Active Learning	0.069
	(0.052)
Gender	−0.051
	(0.063)
Minority	−0.070
	(0.092)
Parent Education	−0.003
	(0.010)
Parent Income	−0.013
	(0.011)
High School Grades	0.040*
	(0.018)
Initial Institutional Commitment	0.089*
	(0.038)
Constant	0.167
	(0.294)
Observations	407
R-squared	0.270

Note: Standard errors in parentheses.

*Significant at .05 level. **Significant at .01 level. ***Significant at .001 level.

initial level of institutional commitment (β = .089, p = .020). Table 5.4 indicates that a student's level of subsequent institutional commitment is positively related to retention. In addition to using ordinary least squares regression to examine this relationship, logistical regression was also employed to examine the impact of subsequent institutional commitment on student retention. These results were positive and statistically significant, indicating that a one-unit increase in a student's subsequent institutional commitment raises the odds of that student's remaining enrolled in the institution the following semester by 3.08 times.

Discussion

The primary goal of this study was to examine the impact of active learning on a student's level of overall social integration and perception of his or her institution's commitment to student welfare. In addition, this study looked at the relationship of a student's social integration, level of subsequent institutional commitment, and persistence. This research extends the previous work of Braxton, Milem, and Sullivan (2000) in its use a multi-institutional sample along with an actual measure of student persistence (as opposed to

Table 5.4. OLS Estimates of the Impact of Subsequent Institutional Commitment on Student Retention

Subsequent Institutional Commitment	0.111***
	(0.026)
Social Integration	0.034
	(0.039)
Institutional Commitment to Student Welfare	−0.045
	(0.040)
Active Learning	−0.011
	(0.027)
Gender	−0.026
	(0.033)
Minority	−0.068
	(0.048)
Parent Education	0.010
	(0.005)
Parent Income	−0.005
	(0.006)
High School Grades	0.003
	(0.009)
Initial Institutional Commitment	0.034
	(0.020)
Constant	0.371*
	(0.152)
Observations	407
R-squared	0.120

Note: Standard errors in parentheses.

*Significant at .05 level. **Significant at .01 level. ***Significant at .001 level

a proxy measure) and the use of a composite variable to measure student perceptions of faculty use of active learning principles.

Our findings support three of this study's four directional hypothesis. The positive relationship between active learning and student perception of the institution's commitment to student welfare indicates that pedagogical practices that encourage students to engage in doing and thinking during class as opposed to passively listening influences students' belief about how much their institution cares about their success. However, this study's second hypothesis was not supported; we failed to find a statistically significant relationship between active learning and a student's level of social integration. As suggested by the results of model II displayed in Table 5.2, the influence of active learning on social integration may be moderated by the direct effect of the commitment of the institution to student welfare on social integration.

The positive relationship between social integration and a student's subsequent level of institutional commitment and the positive relationship between a student's subsequent level of institutional commitment and their likelihood of persistence is consistent with theoretical formulations (Tinto,

1975; Braxton, Hirschy, and McClendon, 2004). Both of these findings add to the extensive body of evidence indicating the highly reliable nature of these two relationships (Braxton and Lee, 2005).

Limitations

As with most other research, the results of this study are modified by a couple of limitations. Our sample is limited to residential, religiously affiliated colleges and universities. As a result, the generalizability of this study to other colleges and universities is somewhat limited. The 28.4 percent rate of response to the survey across the eight participating colleges and universities constitutes another limitation. However, this limitation is obviated to some extent by the weighting of survey responses in two institutions by gender and race to ensure some degree of representativeness to their respective campus populations.

Conclusion and Recommendations for Practice

Faculty use of active learning practices plays a significant role in the retention of first-year college students. This assertion forms the primary conclusion of this study, which lends support to a similar conclusion that Braxton, Milem, and Sullivan (2000) advanced. The pattern of findings of this study tends to indicate that active learning practices that faculty use shape in students the perception that their college or university is committed to their welfare in general and their growth and development in particular, a perception that leads to their sense of social integration. The greater a student's degree of social integration, the greater is his or her level of subsequent commitment to the college or university. The greater the student's level of subsequent commitment to the college or university, the greater is his or her likelihood of persistence in the college or university of initial choice. Thus, active learning plays an indirect but formative role in the retention of first-year college students.

We offer four recommendations for institutional practice:

- Individuals responsible for faculty development activities should develop workshops and seminars focused on assisting faculty members in the development of active learning practices. Braxton, Milem, and Sullivan (2000) also advanced this recommendation. The development of active learning activities requires that faculty acquire new skills given that lecturing, a passive form of instruction, prevails as the primary mode of instruction: more than three-fourths (76.2 percent) of college and university faculty members use it as their primary method of instruction (Finkelstein, Seal, and Schuster, 1998). The skills of active learning emphasized in this study include fostering class discussion of course ideas and concepts and faculty questions posed to students in class that require higher-order thinking to respond.

NEW DIRECTIONS FOR TEACHING AND LEARNING • DOI: 10.1002/tl

- Faculty use of active learning practices in their courses should carry some weight in the assessment of faculty teaching performance for reappointment, tenure, and promotion decisions. Annual faculty salary decisions should also give some consideration to the use of active learning practices by faculty members in their courses.
- Individuals who advise first-year students in the selection of their courses should encourage their advisees to enroll in courses, when possible, in which faculty make frequent use of active learning practices. Such academic advisers include faculty members, professional advisers, and peer advisers. This recommendation mirrors and reinforces a suggestion for institutional practice that Braxton, Milem, and Sullivan (2000) advanced.
- Student course rating instruments should include items that ask students how frequently faculty use active learning practices in the focal course, another recommendation that Braxton, Milem, and Sullivan (2000) proposed. The five items used in this study suggest the types of items that course rating instruments might include. The collection of such information is essential for the implementation of the previous two recommendations for practice.

Colleges and universities seeking to reduce their institution's first-year student departure rate should give serious attention to the implementation of these four recommendations for institutional practice. The practices embedded in these recommendations serve as an augmentation to other institutional efforts designed to reduce the unnecessary departure of first-year college students. Moreover, the implementation of these recommendations contributes to student learning because the use of active learning practices by college and university faculty members enhances student knowledge and understanding of course content (Anderson and Adams, 1992; Chickering and Gamson, 1987; Johnson, Johnson, and Smith, 1991; McKeachie, Pintrich, Yi-Guang, and Smith, 1986).

References

Anderson, J. A., and Adams, A. M. "Acknowledging the Learning Styles of Diverse Student Populations: Implications for Instructional Design." In L.L.B. Border and N.V.N. Chism (eds.), *Teaching for Diversity*. New Directions for Teaching and Learning, no. 49. San Francisco: Jossey-Bass, 1992.

Bean, J. P. "Dropouts and Turnover: The Synthesis and Test of a Causal Model of College Student Attrition." *Research in Higher Education*, 1980, *12*, 155–187.

Bean, J. P. "The Application of a Model of Turnover in Work Organizations to the Student Attrition Process." *Review of Higher Education*, 1983, *12*, 155–182.

Bonwell, C. C., and Eison, J. A. *Active Learning: Creating Excitement in the Classroom.* ASHE-ERIC Higher Education Report, no. 1. San Francisco: Jossey-Bass, 1991.

Braxton, J. M. "Toward a Theory of Faculty Professional Choice in Teaching That Fosters College Student Success." In J. C. Smart (ed.), *Higher Education: Handbook of Theory and Research* (vol. 23, pp. 181–207). Dordrecht: Springer, 2008.

Braxton, J. M., Hirschy, A. S., and McClendon, S. A. *Toward Understanding and Reducing College Student Departure.* ASHE-ERIC Higher Education Report, vol. 30, no. 3. San Francisco: Jossey-Bass, 2004.

Braxton, J. M., and Lee, S. D. "Toward Reliable Knowledge About College Student Departure." In A. Seidman (ed.), *College Student Retention: Formula for Student Success.* Westport, Conn.: Praeger, 2005.

Braxton, J. M., Milem, J. F., and Sullivan, A. S. "The Influence of Active Learning on the College Student Departure Process: Toward a Revision of Tinto's Theory." *Journal of Higher Education,* 2000, 71(5), 569–590.

Braxton, J. M., Sullivan, A. S., and Johnson, R. M. "Appraising Tinto's Theory of College Student Departure." In J. C. Smart (ed.), *Higher Education: Handbook of Theory and Research.* New York: Agathon, 1997.

Cabrera, A. F., Castaneda, M. B., Nora, A., and Hengstler, D. "The Convergence Between Two Theories of College Persistence." *Journal of Higher Education,* 1992, 63, 143–164.

Chickering, A. W., and Gamson, Z. F. "Seven Principles for Good Practice." *AAHE Bulletin,* 1987, 39, 3–7.

Finkelstein, M. J., Seal, R. K., and Schuster, J. H. *The New Academic Generation: A Profession in Transformation.* Baltimore, Md.: The Johns Hopkins University Press, 1998.

Johnson, D. W., Johnson, R. T., and Smith, K. A. *Cooperative Learning: Increasing College Faculty Instructional Productivity.* ASHE-ERIC Higher Education Report, no. 4. San Francisco: Jossey-Bass, 1991.

McKeachie, W. J., Pintrich, P. R., Yi-Guang, L., and Smith, D.A.F. *Teaching and Learning in the College Classroom: A Review of the Research Literature.* Ann Arbor: Regents of the University of Michigan, 1986.

Milem, J. F., and Berger, J. B. "A Modified Model of Student Persistence: Exploring the Relationship Between Astin's Theory of Involvement and Tinto's Theory of Student Departure." *Journal of College Student Development,* 1997, 38, 387–400.

Pascarella, E. T., Duby, P., and Iverson, B. "A Test and Reconceptualization of a Theoretical Model of College Withdrawal in a Commuter Institution Setting." *Sociology of Education,* 1983, 56, 88–100.

Sorcinelli, M. D. "Research Findings on the Seven Principles." In A. W. Chickering and Z. F. Gamson (eds.), *Applying the Seven Principles of Good Practice in Undergraduate Education.* San Francisco: Jossey-Bass, 1991.

Tinto, V. "Dropout from Higher Education: A Theoretical Synthesis of Recent Research." *Review of Educational Research,* 1975, 45, 89–125.

Voorhees, R. "Toward Building Models of Community College Persistence: A Logit Analysis." *Research in Higher Education,* 1987, 16, 115–129.

JOHN M. BRAXTON *is professor of education in the Higher Education Leadership and Policy Program, Department of Leadership, Policy and Organizations of Peabody College at Vanderbilt University.*

WILLIS A. JONES *is a doctoral student in the Higher Education Leadership and Policy Program, Department of Leadership, Policy and Organizations of Peabody College at Vanderbilt University.*

AMY S. HIRSCHY *is assistant professor in the College of Education and Human Development at the University of Louisville.*

HAROLD V. HARTLEY III *is senior vice president of the Council of Independent Colleges, Washington, D.C.*

NEW DIRECTIONS FOR TEACHING AND LEARNING • DOI: 10.1002/tl

6

This chapter discusses the finding that student retention benefits when the instruction increases the level of academic challenge and the amount of support provided to students.

Classroom Practices at Institutions with Higher-Than-Expected Persistence Rates: What Student Engagement Data Tell Us

Thomas F. Nelson Laird, Daniel Chen, George D. Kuh

For decades, the national college graduation rate has hovered around 50 percent (Astin, 1975; Braxton, 2000; Pascarella and Terenzini, 2005; Tinto, 1993). Baccalaureate completion rates at individual institutions vary considerably, with more than four-fifths of students at some selective colleges earning a degree after four years, while at about a fifth of four-year institutions, less than one-third of first-time full-time students do so within six years (Carey, 2004). Even if these estimates are low, as some claim (Adelman, 2004), everyone agrees that persistence and educational attainment rates, as well as the quality of student learning, must improve if postsecondary education is to meet the needs of our nation and the rest of the world. Indeed, some predict that as many as four-fifths of high school graduates need some form of postsecondary education to manage the increasingly volatile and complex economic, social, political, and cultural issues they will face (Kazis, Vargas, and Hoffman, 2004; McCabe, 2000). In addition, over the course of a lifetime, college graduates continue to earn on average $1 million more than people with only a high school diploma, making college a very good financial investment (Pennington, 2004).

Unfortunately, the odds of succeeding in college are stacked against certain types of students. Disproportionate numbers of those who drop out are from historically underserved groups. No wonder clarion calls to improve the

NEW DIRECTIONS FOR TEACHING AND LEARNING, no. 115, Fall 2008 © Wiley Periodicals, Inc.
Published online in Wiley InterScience (www.interscience.wiley.com) • DOI: 10.1002/tl.327

quality of undergraduate education are coming from every corner: campus leaders, policymakers, government officials, and higher education associations.

Decades ago, when undergraduates were from more homogeneous backgrounds and most lived on campus near their classmates and teachers, propinquity and serendipity established the social order and helped to inculcate shared values and understandings. Today, students are more diverse in almost every way. The majority of students commute to school, with most working at some point during their studies, some many hours a week. For these students and nontrivial numbers who attend so-called residential campuses but live off-campus, the classroom is the only venue where they regularly have face-to-face contact with faculty or staff members and other students. This means that classroom learning environments and teaching and learning practices are ever more important, all of which makes the instructor's job more demanding and complicated. Faculty must cultivate an atmosphere in which strangers need to learn how to listen critically and attentively, interact effectively with others, and challenge and support one another to high levels of academic performance (Kuh and others, 2007). To respond productively, we need to better understand the relationships between classroom practices and desired outcomes of college.

The best predictors of whether a student will graduate are academic preparation and motivation (Adelman, 2004; Pascarella and Terenzini, 1991, 2005). What can colleges and universities do after students arrive to increase the chances they will find their studies fulfilling, persist, and graduate? Decades of research studies on college impact and persistence suggest that student engagement is a promising area of emphasis.

Why Student Engagement Matters

At the institutional level, effective educational practices such as active and collaborative learning and student-faculty interaction are associated with higher grades and greater student self-reported educational gains (Kuh, 2007; National Survey of Student Engagement, 2006; Pascarella and Terenzini, 2005). This is because what students do during college counts more in terms of what they learn and whether they will persist in college compared with their background characteristics or where they go to college (Astin, 1993; Pascarella and Terenzini, 1991; Pace, 1980). Certain institutional practices are known to lead to high levels of student engagement (Astin, 1991; Chickering and Reisser, 1993; Kuh and Associates, 2005; Pascarella and Terenzini, 2005), with the best-known set of engagement indicators being Chickering and Gamson's seven principles for good practice in undergraduate education (1987): student-faculty contact, cooperation among students, active learning, prompt feedback, time on task, high expectations, and respect for diverse talents and ways of learning. Also important to student learning are learning environments that students perceive to be inclusive and affirming and where expectations for performance are clearly communicated and set at reasonably high levels (Education

Commission of the States, 1995; Kuh, 2001; Kuh and Associates, 2005; Pascarella, 2001).

Because "individual effort and involvement are the critical determinants of college impact" (Pascarella and Terenzini, 2005, p. 602), colleges and universities must find ways to encourage student engagement inside and outside the classroom. Lee Shulman (2007), president emeritus of the Carnegie Foundation for the Advancement of Teaching, says that student engagement is both a proxy for learning and a desired outcome in itself. By being engaged, students develop habits that promise to stand them in good stead for a lifetime of continuous learning. In addition, some recent studies show that engagement has compensatory effects: students who start college less advantaged tend to benefit more in terms of their grades, for example, than higher-achieving students (Cruce, Wolniak, Seifert, and Pascarella, 2006; Kuh and others, 2007).

Student engagement has two key components. The first is the amount of time and effort students put into their studies and other activities and experiences associated with the outcomes that constitute student success. The second is how the institution allocates resources and organizes learning opportunities and services to induce students to participate in and benefit from such activities. The teaching and learning approaches that faculty members use are of particular interest, as those are the classroom practices and student behaviors over which an institution has some direct influence. That is, if faculty members use principles of good practice to design assignments and engaging pedagogies to structure in-class and out-of-class activities, students would ostensibly put forth more effort. They would write more papers, read more books, meet more frequently with faculty and peers, and use information technology appropriately, all of which would result in greater gains in such areas as critical thinking, problem solving, effective communication, and responsible citizenship.

Assuming that faculty can more frequently and effectively use practices that get students to participate in educationally purposeful activities, where might we look to see if such efforts pay dividends in terms of persistence?

In the business world, a time-honored approach to improving effectiveness is identifying and adapting the practices of high-performing organizations. This was the premise of Jim Collins's best seller, *From Good to Great* (2001), and other books profiling excellent businesses and industries (Peters and Waterman, 1982). With a similar aim in mind, Kuh and Associates (2005) studied twenty high-performing four-year colleges and universities thought to "add value" to their students' experiences by virtue of having higher-than-predicted graduation rates and higher-than-predicted scores on NSSE measures. The presumption was that such educationally effective colleges and universities channel students' energies toward appropriate activities and engage them at a high level in these activities (Education Commission of the States, 1995; Study Group on the Conditions of Excellence in American Higher Education, 1984). Using similar logic, we would expect that at institutions where faculty members more often use engaging pedagogies, students at these institutions would consequently participate more frequently in educationally effective activities, which would have the salutary effect of fostering higher levels of student success, including persistence. Whether this is in fact the case is not clear because relatively few inquiries have focused on the relationship between engaging classroom practices and persistence.

Using the institution as the unit of analysis, this chapter examines persistence rates for hundreds of institutions that have administered NSSE. A model predicting persistence with institutional and aggregated student characteristics was used to determine two groups of institutions: those that are doing better than expected and those doing as expected in terms of undergraduate student persistence rates. Student engagement was compared between the two groups to determine the links between doing better than expected and effective educational practices, particularly practices connected to the classroom. We also compared faculty practices between the better-than-expected and as-expected institutions by limiting our sample of institutions further to those that have administered the Faculty Survey of Student Engagement (FSSE).

Better-Than-Expected Persistence

First, we had to identify the institutions that had higher-than-expected persistence rates using U.S. institutions that participated in NSSE at least once from 2003 to 2007. We pulled information from the Integrated Postsecondary Education Data System to create the variables for each institution. Only institutions with valid values for each measure were retained in our analysis, which resulted in a sample of 924 baccalaureate degree-granting institutions.

We used a regression model to predict the rate at which full-time first-year students at each institution returned for the second year. Based on previous research (Braxton, 2000; Pascarella and Terenzini, 1991, 2005) and theory (Tinto, 1993; Pascarella, 1985), we used institutional characteristics such as undergraduate enrollment and cost and aggregated student background characteristics such as percentage of full-time students to predict persistence rates. The model explained over 62 percent of the variance in persistence rates.

We were less interested in confirming the institutional indicators of persistence and more interested in identifying institutions that were doing better than expected, which for our purposes meant institutions where the actual persistence rate was five or more points above the persistence rate predicted by the model. For comparison purposes, we also identified those institutions doing as expected—institutions with actual persistence rates within five points of their predicted persistence rates.

By focusing on institutions doing better than expected, the investigation shifts to recognizing that an institution is unlikely to change its persistence rate by twenty points, for example. That would almost require becoming a different type of institution serving different types of students.

An institution is much more likely to make, and should be more interested in, meaningful change on the margin, particularly in the near term.

As it turned out, 570 were doing as expected and 174 institutions doing better than expected. So what explains an institution's better-than-expected performance? While this question deserves in-depth study beyond the scope of this chapter, our supposition—based on previous work on compensatory effects and effective campus practices (Cruce, Wolniak, Seifert, and Pascarella, 2006; Kuh and Associates, 2005)—was that better-than-expected persistence would be positively connected to student engagement and the frequency with which faculty members used effective educational practices. Indeed, we found that campuses with higher-than-expected persistence had higher levels of student engagement in classroom-related areas such as academic challenge and active and collaborative learning and that faculty on those campuses reported emphasizing effective practices more in their courses.

We attempted to identify differences between the two groups of institutions by comparing average first-year student scores on four of the five NSSE clusters of effective educational practice listed in Table 6.1. Each engagement measure was based on only first-year student responses, because persistence, as measured in this and most other studies, is largely a first-year phenomenon. The enriching educational experiences measure is not used because a number of its items focus on experiences students do not participate in until later in their academic career, such as capstone experiences, study abroad, and internships.

To look for differences in student engagement between institutions with better-than-expected persistence rates and those with as-expected persistence rates, we first standardized each institutional indicator of engagement (converted the scores so that the mean for the 744 institutions was zero and the standard deviation was 1). Then, using t-tests with a minimum threshold for statistical significance set as alpha = 0.05, we compared the means for each group of institutions, noting which group scored higher and testing to see if the mean differences were statistically significant. By standardizing the measures, the resulting mean differences were interpretable as effect sizes, which aids in judging the magnitude of the differences.

Indicators of Student Engagement

In the following section, we describe each engagement indicator used in our analyses and discuss how institutions with better-than-expected persistence rates differ from institutions with as-expected rates of persistence.

Academic Challenge. This indicator includes the amount of reading and writing students do for their courses, the amount of emphasis their courses place on higher-order thinking skills such as analysis and synthesis, working hard to meet an instructor's expectations, the amount of time students spend per week preparing for their courses, and students' perceptions

Table 6.1. Aggregate Engagement and Faculty Practice Indicators

Name	Description (Source)
First-year students	
Level of academic challenge	Reading and writing for courses, emphasis of course work on higher-order thinking skills as well as student time on task, and effort (NSSE)
Active and collaborative learning	In- and out-of-class participation in discussion, presentation, and group activities (NSSE)
Student-faculty interaction	In- and out-of-class discussion with faculty, feedback from faculty, and work with faculty outside course work (NSSE)
Supportive campus environment	Institutional emphasis on support and the quality of student relationships with other students, faculty, and administration (NSSE)
Faculty teaching lower-division courses	
Deep approaches to learning	Emphasis placed on higher-order and integrative learning in courses (FSSE)
Active classroom practice	Time spent in class on small group work, in-class writing, student presentations, and teacher-student led activities (FSSE)
Faculty-student contact	Contact with students in their courses by e-mail and about grades and career plans (FSSE)
Intellectual skills	Courses structured to emphasize writing and speaking clearly, analyzing problems, and learning on one's own (FSSE)
Practical skills	Courses structured to emphasize solving real-world problems, working with others, job skills, and computer use (FSSE)
Individual and social responsibility	Courses structured to emphasize understanding one's self and people of other racial and ethnic backgrounds (FSSE)

Note: All variables in table were continuous and standardized prior to analysis. For component items, see National Survey of Student Engagement (2007) and Nelson Laird, Niskodé, and Kuh (2006).

of their institutions' emphasis on spending significant amounts of time studying. The higher an institution scores on this item, the more work students on that campus are doing for their courses and the more those courses focus on thinking skills beyond simple memorization.

On average, the level of academic challenge reported by first-year students was higher at institutions with better-than-expected persistence rates than at institutions with persistence rates that were close to expected. The difference was nearly two-tenths of a standard deviation (Table 6.2), which

Table 6.2. Comparing First-Year Student Engagement Levels and Lower-Division Faculty Practices by Institutional Group

	Means Group 1[a]	Group 2[a]	Mean Difference
Indicators of student engagement			
Level of academic challenge	0.14	−0.04	0.19*
Active and collaborative learning	0.24	−0.07	0.32**
Student-faculty interaction	0.09	−0.03	0.12
Supportive campus environment	0.25	−0.07	0.32**
Indicators of faculty teaching practices			
Deep approaches to learning	0.04	−0.01	0.06
Active classroom practice	0.21	−0.06	0.27†
Faculty-student contact	−0.01	0.00	−0.02
Intellectual skills	0.22	−0.06	0.28*
Practical skills	0.24	−0.07	0.31*
Individual and social responsibility	0.16	−0.05	0.21

Note: All measures standardized prior to analysis making the mean difference an effect size estimate.

[a]Group 1 = Institutions with better-than-expected persistence (N = 174 for student engagement measures and 66 for faculty practice measures). Group 2 = institutions with as-expected persistence (N = 570 for student engagement measures and 224 for faculty practice measures).

†$p < 0.10$, *$p < 0.05$. **$p < 0.001$.

is modest but hardly negligible. This result suggests that compared to their counterparts at institutions with as-expected persistence rates, first-year students report doing more academic work and their courses emphasize more complex levels of thinking at institutions that beat the odds and have higher-than-expected persistence.

Active and Collaborative Learning. This indicator shows the amount students are actively participating in class by asking questions, giving presentations, or working on in-class projects with other students, as well as the amount of collaborative experiences such as working on assignments with classmates outside class, tutoring, working on a community-based project for a course, or having discussions with others outside class about course-related material. As with academic challenge, this indicator represents students' classroom experiences that are shaped to a large degree by how faculty members structure class time and assignments.

The average institutional score on active and collaborative learning was higher at institutions with higher-than-expected persistence compared with institutions with as-expected persistence. The difference was nearly one-third of a standard deviation (Table 6.2), a moderately sized gap. This result suggests that in general, first-year students at institutions with higher-than-expected persistence are more actively participating in class and doing more collaborative academic work with their peers than are their counterparts at institutions with as-expected persistence.

Student-Faculty Interaction. This indicator combines course-related interactions such as discussing grades, discussing ideas and readings outside class, and receiving prompt feedback with items divorced from course work such as talking about career plans or working on noncourse activities such as committees or orientation. The student-faculty interaction benchmark contains an item about student research with a faculty member that is not included in this study because the item changed during the years from which we pulled the engagement indicators.

We found that student-faculty interaction is, on average, slightly higher (about a tenth of a standard deviation Table 6.2) at institutions with better-than-expected persistence than at institutions with persistence rates near expected. While slightly higher, the difference is not statistically significant, suggesting that we should not be confident that the real difference between these institutions is greater or less than zero. In essence, the institutional level of student-faculty interaction is roughly equal for the two groups of institutions.

Supportive Campus Environment. This is the indicator least directly connected to classroom practice: it comprises items that focus on the quality of students' relationships with other students, faculty, and administrative offices and personnel. It also contains items about the extent to which students perceive that the campus provides the academic and nonacademic support they need to succeed. While the connection to the classroom is distal, this institution-level measure reflects in part the support students feel they receive in their classes. That is, students likely base their judgments about the quality of their relationships with faculty on classroom interactions and activities.

The average institution with a better-than-expected persistence rate scored higher on supportive campus environment than the average institution with an as-expected persistence rate. As with active and collaborative learning, the difference was nearly a third of a standard deviation (Table 6.2), indicating a moderate difference. It follows that first-year students at institutions with better-than-expected persistence rates feel they are getting more academic and social support compared with their counterparts at colleges and universities with near-expected persistence rates.

Summary of Student Engagement Findings. Overall, better-than-expected institutions provide higher levels of academic challenge and support than institutions with as-expected persistence, a result that echoes the calls from student development scholars that colleges seek to balance these two key learning conditions (Baxter Magolda, 2001; Kegan, 1994; King and Kitchener, 1994; Perry, 1970; Sanford, 1962). We also found that the average level of active and collaborative engagement in academic endeavors is higher on campuses doing better than expected in terms of persistence, something that corroborates findings that link active and collaborative practices with student outcomes including persistence and graduation (Braxton, Milem, and Sullivan, 2000).

NEW DIRECTIONS FOR TEACHING AND LEARNING • DOI: 10.1002/tl

Indicators of Faculty Practices

The information from students suggests that classroom activities and environments are positively linked with better-than-expected persistence rates. However, students are not the only source of information about what happens in college and university classrooms. Consequently, the next analytical step was to examine responses from college and university faculty at the two groups of institutions.

Because not all NSSE institutions participate in FSSE, the sample of eligible institutions shrank to 66 with better-than-expected persistence rates and 224 with as-expected rates. Similar to the analyses based on NSSE measures, we focused on faculty teaching lower-division courses—those taught primarily to first-year students and sophomores. At these 290 institutions, faculty respondents to FSSE answered a series of questions with the frame of reference being a single course of their choosing that they taught during the current academic year. Six FSSE measures were aggregated to create institution-level indicators of faculty emphasis on deep approaches to learning, active classroom practices, faculty-student contact, and three clusters of essential learning outcomes that are proxies for several "essential 21st century competencies" described by the Association of American Colleges and Universities (2007): intellectual skills, practical skills, and individual and social responsibility (Table 6.1). As with the student engagement indicators, each measure was standardized, and t-tests were used to compare mean differences among the groups. Due to the relatively small sample of institutions for this part of the analysis, we note statistical significance for alpha set as high as 0.10.

Deep Approaches to Learning. The degree to which faculty emphasize deep approaches to learning represents what faculty do to structure their courses to promote higher-order thinking skills such as analysis and synthesis, and integrating learning across contexts and in dialogue with others. Because of the higher-order learning items, this measure both empirically and conceptually overlaps with the student measure of academic challenge. At the institution level, this represents the academic rigor of course work and the degree to which faculty-designed activities emphasize deep as contrasted with surface types of learning and understanding.

On average, faculty members in institutions with better-than-expected persistence rates emphasize deep approaches to learning in lower-division courses to about the same degree as faculty in schools with as-expected persistence (Table 6.2). In fact, the former scores above the latter by only six one-hundredths of a standard deviation, perhaps because faculty at these two sets of institutions on average expect roughly the same level of academic rigor.

Faculty use of active classroom practices indicates how much time faculty devote to small group work, in-class writing, student presentations, and teacher-student led activities, all of which limit the amount of time they lecture. At the institutional level, this is an indicator of how much faculty members teaching lower-division courses use active rather than passive forms of instruction.

Institutions with better-than-expected persistence have faculty members whose use of active classroom practices is on average over a quarter of a standard deviation higher than faculty members in those institutions with as-expected persistence (Table 6.2). This finding mirrors the fact that students are engaged in more active and collaborative learning activities at institutions with better-than-expected persistence relative to the other institutions. More frequent faculty use of such practices has been linked to students' reporting more often doing such activities (Kuh, Nelson Laird, and Umbach, 2004; Umbach and Wawrzynski, 2005). The results of our analysis also suggest that faculty use of active learning practices may have salutary effects on student persistence. The probability that this difference is due to chance is less than 10 percent, a threshold for statistical significance that seems adequate given the relatively small number of institutions in the sample.

Faculty-Student Contact. This indicator refers to the percentages of students in faculty members' courses who occasionally use e-mail to contact them, occasionally discuss grades, and talk with them at least once about career plans. This item and the NSSE student-faculty interaction measure are really two sides of the same coin, particularly at the institution level where the FSSE measure represents the amount faculty perceive they are interacting with students and the NSSE measure represents students' perceptions of how often they interact with faculty.

As with the NSSE results, the two sets of institutions had nearly identical average levels of faculty-student contact based on responses from lower-division faculty (Table 6.2). The difference is about two one-hundredths of a standard deviation, with better-than-expected institutions scoring slightly lower than as-expected institutions. So although student-faculty contact has been found to positively affect persistence at the individual student level (Pascarella and Terenzini, 1991, 2005; Tinto, 1993), we did not find a similar relationship between student-faculty contact and persistence at the institution level.

Intellectual Skills. The emphasis faculty give to intellectual skills represents how they structure their courses so that students learn and have opportunities to develop their abilities to write and speak clearly and effectively, as well as think critically, analyze problems, and learn on their own. At the institution level, this is an indicator of how much the course work at a college or university is focused on promoting intellectual development.

The typical better-than-expected institution emphasizes this type of outcome more in its lower-division courses (Table 6.2). The difference is greater than a quarter of a standard deviation and suggests a moderate but meaningful gap between the two types of institutions, suggesting that better-than-expected institutions place more emphasis on students' acquiring these skills and competencies in lower-division courses.

Practical Skills. The amount that faculty emphasize practical skills indicates the extent to which they structure their courses to give students opportunities to solve complex, real-world problems and work effectively with others, as well as work on computer and job skills. Faculty members in better-than-expected institutions scored nearly one-third of a standard deviation higher on average than faculty members in the as-expected institutions on their emphasis of practical skills in their courses (Table 6.2).

Individual and Social Responsibility. Faculty can promote individual and social responsibility by arranging class-based activities and assignments that focus on self-understanding and understanding people of other racial and ethnic backgrounds. Institutions with better-than-expected persistence scored higher on average on this measure, although the 0.21 standard deviation difference was not statistically significant. It may be instructive to conduct this analysis again in a few more years with a larger number of institutions that have NSSE and FSSE data.

Discussion and Conclusions

Institutional efforts to improve persistence have largely focused on developing such programs and activities as summer bridge programs, intensive orientation, first-year seminars, learning communities, and intrusive advising that are designed to prepare students for what is to come and help them acquire the academic skills needed to survive. Students at risk of dropping out are sometimes required to participate in such programs and activities. For individual students or certain subgroups of students, these approaches sometimes have had the intended results (Pascarella and Terenzini, 2005). In general, most of these interventions emphasize actively involving students in their academic experiences while providing them with the necessary support when they encounter problems.

Such efforts have two common features. First, they are structured to promote student engagement in educationally purposeful activities outside the classroom, which have the salutary effect of shrinking the psychological size of the institution. Such efforts are necessary but far from sufficient; as Astin (1977) pointed out decades ago, one of the worst public policy decisions in terms of student success was allowing—even encouraging— undergraduate enrollments to swell beyond fifteen to twenty thousand students because increasing size is anathema to student success. Second, efforts to boost persistence rates typically focus on doing something to or for the student. The findings of this study suggest that to improve persistence, institutions might also try to modify the nature of early academic experiences in all classes to enhance student engagement, and not just expect a first-year seminar or learning community to make up for deficiencies in productive learning conditions in other course offerings. Although much more work is needed to determine what practices are effective in particular institutional contexts, our findings suggest some meaningful next steps and questions.

New Directions for Teaching and Learning • DOI: 10.1002/tl

Implications for College Classrooms

The results of this study suggest an institution-level analogue to the assertion that a student's development is a function of an optimal blend of challenge and support (Kegan, 1994; Sanford, 1962). Institutions with better-than-expected persistence had higher levels of academic challenge and were viewed by students as more supportive, on average, compared to institutions with as-expected persistence rates. The implication is to simultaneously ratchet up the level of academic challenge as well as the amount of support provided to students. Meeting students where they are in terms of their academic preparation, developmental level, and motivation and finding ways to help them succeed is a complex task to be sure, one deserving greater attention from researchers and practitioners.

Toward this end, institutions could start by answering some context-specific questions similar to those posed by Kuh, Kinzie, Schuh, and Whitt (2005). For example, what courses taught by which faculty are best equipped to appropriately stretch students to previously unattainable levels of performance? Our findings suggest that raising the level of challenge in the first year may help, but should it be in all lower-division courses or a coupling of general education courses and particular courses for each major? Alternatively, a campus could consider analyzing its curriculum and its methods of advising to determine if the overall level of challenge at the institution could be raised by better matching individual students to programs of study that are appropriately challenging. What areas of the institution should provide students with support? Should the classroom be a primary vehicle for providing support? If yes, what kinds of support?

Interestingly, we did not find much of a difference in faculty emphasis on deep approaches to learning between the two groups of institutions. This apparent mismatch with the student findings about academic challenge suggests that correctly pitching course offerings to students' level is necessary for student success. Perhaps faculty and staff at better-than-expected institutions are better at blending challenge and support than their counterparts at the as-expected institutions.

The findings also suggest that campuses with better-than-expected persistence place more emphasis on the social and collaborative aspects of learning. In terms of both the student- and faculty-aggregated measures of active and collaborative learning, the better-than-expected institutions had higher scores on active learning in the classroom and more collaboration on academic tasks in and out of the classroom. This is consistent with student-level investigations (Braxton, Milem, and Sullivan, 2000) and is compatible with philosophies of education that view student learning and development as inherently a social process (Vygotsky, 1962, 1978). From such a perspective, active and collaborative learning practices are especially important in the first college year because they serve as a crosswalk between the institution's academic and social systems (Tinto, 1993), an overlap that

NEW DIRECTIONS FOR TEACHING AND LEARNING • DOI: 10.1002/tl

is not often represented in the most frequently used theories of student departure and socialization.

Finally, institutions wishing to improve persistence need to consider to what degree and to what ends faculty are structuring their courses for first-year students. The aggregated faculty responses in this study suggest that at institutions with better-than-predicted persistence rates, faculty teaching lower-division courses place more emphasis on all three essential learning outcomes: intellectual skills, practical skills, and individual and social responsibility. Currently the emphasis on these essential learning outcomes is not spread evenly across the curriculum. For example, general education courses (GECs) focus on intellectual skills and individual and social responsibility to a greater extent than non-GECs, and the opposite is true for practical skills (Nelson Laird, Niskodé, and Kuh, 2006). However, is this ideal? If an institution wants to ratchet up its emphasis on essential learning outcomes in the first year, should that institution rely primarily on its GECs courses, or should it work to have these outcomes emphasized equally across the curriculum?

Considering the connections between the nature of college and university course offerings and student persistence emerging from this study, institutions wishing to improve student persistence should examine whether and how their courses, particularly lower-division courses, present appropriate levels of academic challenge and engage students in active and collaborative learning activities within a classroom environment in which students feel supported enough to meet the challenges they face. In addition, these early college courses should be focused on what the Association of American Colleges and Universities (2007) calls essential learning outcomes. Attempts to enhance the quality of the student experience in this way is a challenging task for institutions that demands the active involvement of many institutional actors—students and faculty as well as academic and student affairs administrators—in order to realize higher levels of student engagement and success.

References

Adelman, C. *Principal Indicators of Student Academic Histories in Postsecondary Education, 1972–2000.* Washington, D.C.: U.S. Department of Education, Institute of Education Sciences, 2004.

Association of American Colleges and Universities. *College Learning for the New Global Century.* Washington, D.C.: Association of American Colleges and Universities, 2007.

Astin, A. W. *The Power of Protest: A National Study of Student and Faculty Disruptions with Implications for the Future.* San Francisco: Jossey-Bass. 1975.

Astin, A. W. *Four Critical Years: Effects of College on Beliefs, Attitudes, and Knowledge.* San Francisco: Jossey-Bass, 1977.

Astin, A. W. "The Changing American College Student: Implications for Educational Policy and Practice." *Higher Education,* 1991, 22(2), 129–143.

Astin, A. W. *What Matters in College? Four Critical Years Revisited.* San Francisco: Jossey-Bass, 1993.

Baxter Magolda, M. B. *Making Their Own Way: Narratives for Transforming Higher Education to Promote Self-Development.* Sterling, Va.: Stylus, 2001.

Braxton, J. M. (ed.). *Reworking the Student Departure Puzzle.* Nashville, Tenn.: Vanderbilt University Press, 2000.

Braxton, J. M., Milem, J. F., and Sullivan, A. S. "The Influence of Active Learning on the College Student Departure Process: Toward a Revision of Tinto's theory." *Journal of Higher Education,* 2000, 71(5), 569–590.

Carey, K. *A Matter of Degrees: Improving Graduation Rates in Four-Year Colleges and Universities.* Washington, D.C.: Education Trust, 2004.

Chickering, A. W., and Gamson, Z. F. "Seven Principles for Good Practice in Undergraduate Education." *AAHE Bulletin,* 1987, 39, 3–7.

Chickering, A. W., and Reisser, L. *Education and Identity.* (2nd ed.) San Francisco: Jossey-Bass, 1993.

Collins, J. C. *Good to Great: Why Some Companies Make the Leap—and Others Don't.* New York: HarperBusiness, 2001.

Cruce, T. M., Wolniak, G. C., Seifert, T. A., and Pascarella, E. T. "Impacts of Good Practices on Cognitive Development, Learning Orientations, and Graduate Degree Plans During the First Year of College." *Journal of College Student Development,* 2006, 9(4), 365–383.

Education Commission of the States. *Making Quality Count in Undergraduate Education.* Denver, Colo.: ECS Distribution Center, 1995.

Kazis, R., Vargas, J., and Hoffman, N. *Double the Numbers: Increasing Postsecondary Credentials for Underrepresented Youth.* Cambridge, Mass.: Harvard Education Press, 2004.

Kegan, R. *In over Our Heads: The Mental Demands of Modern Life.* Cambridge, Mass.: Harvard University Press, 1994.

King, P., and Kitchener, K. *Developing Reflective Judgment: Understanding and Promoting Intellectual Growth and Critical Thinking in Adolescents and Adults.* San Francisco: Jossey-Bass, 1994.

Kuh, G. D. "Assessing What Really Matters to Student Learning: Inside the National Survey of Student Engagement." *Change,* 2001, 33(3), 10–17, 66.

Kuh, G. D. "Risky Business: Promises and Pitfalls of Institutional Transparency." *Change,* 2007, 39(5), 30–35.

Kuh, G. D., and Associates. *Student Success in College: Creating Conditions That Matter.* San Francisco: Jossey-Bass, 2005.

Kuh, G. D., Kinzie, J., Schuh, J. H., and Whitt, E. J. *Assessing Conditions to Enhance Educational Effectiveness: The Inventory for Student Engagement and Success.* San Francisco: Jossey-Bass, 2005.

Kuh, G. D., Nelson Laird, T. F., and Umbach, P. D. "Aligning Faculty Activities and Student Behavior: Realizing the Promise of Greater Expectations." *Liberal Education,* 2004, 90(4), 24–31.

Kuh, G. D., and others. *Piecing Together the Student Success Puzzle: Research, Propositions, and Recommendations.* ASHE Higher Education Report, vol. 32, no. 5. San Francisco: Jossey-Bass, 2007.

McCabe, R. H. *No One to Waste: A Report to Public Decision-Makers and Community College Leaders.* Washington, D.C.: American Association of Community Colleges, 2000.

National Survey of Student Engagement. *Engaged Learning: Fostering Success for All Students.* Bloomington, Ind.: Indiana University Center for Postsecondary Research, 2006.

Nelson Laird, T. F., Niskodé, A. S., and Kuh, G. D. "General Education Courses and the Promotion of Essential Learning Outcomes." Paper presented at the Annual Meeting of the Association for the Study of Higher Education, Anaheim, Calif., Nov. 2006

Pace, C. R. "Measuring the Quality of Student Effort." *Current Issues in Higher Education,* 1980, 2, 10–16.

Pascarella, E. T. "College Environmental Influences on Learning and Cognitive Development: A Critical Review and Synthesis." In J. C. Smart (ed.), *Higher Education: Handbook of Theory and Research*. New York: Agathon, 1985.

Pascarella, E. T. "Cognitive Growth in College: Surprising and Reassuring Findings." *Change*, 2001, 33(6), 20–27.

Pascarella, E. T., and Terenzini, P. T. *How College Affects Students: Findings and Insights from Twenty-Years of Research*. San Francisco: Jossey-Bass, 1991.

Pascarella, E. T., and Terenzini, P. T. *How College Affects Students: A Third Decade of Research*. San Francisco: Jossey-Bass, 2005.

Pennington, H. *Fast Track to College: Increasing Postsecondary Success for All Students*. Boston: Jobs for the Future, 2004.

Perry, W. G. *Forms of Intellectual and Ethical Development in the College Years*. New York: Holt, 1970.

Peters, T., and Waterman, R. H., Jr. *In Search of Excellence*. New York: HarperCollins, 1982.

Sanford, N. (ed.). *The American College*. Hoboken, N.J.: Wiley, 1962.

Shulman, L. S. "Counting and Recounting: Assessment and the Quest for Accountability." *Change*, 2007, 39(1), 20–25.

Study Group on the Conditions of Excellence in Higher Education. *Involvement in Learning: Realizing the Potential of Higher Education*. Washington, D.C.: National Institute of Education, 1984.

Tinto, V. *Leaving College: Rethinking the Causes and Cures of Student Attrition*. (2nd ed.) Chicago: University of Chicago Press, 1993.

Umbach, P. D., and Wawrzynski, M. R. "Faculty Do Matter: The Role of College Faculty in Student Learning and Engagement." *Research in Higher Education*, 2005, 46(2), 153–184.

Vygotsky, L. *Thought and Language*. Cambridge, Mass.: MIT Press, 1962.

Vygotsky, L. *Mind in Society: The Development of Higher Psychological Processes*. Cambridge, Mass.: Harvard University Press, 1978.

THOMAS F. NELSON LAIRD is an assistant professor at Indiana University.

DANIEL CHEN is an assistant professor at the University of North Texas.

GEORGE D. KUH is Chancellor's Professor of Higher Education and director of the Indiana University Center for Postsecondary Research.

7

This chapter provides support for a scholarship of practice focused on the translation of research findings into recommendations for policy and practice designed to increase institutional rates of student retention.

Toward a Scholarship of Practice Centered on College Student Retention

John M. Braxton

Colleges and universities seeking a reduction in their institutional rates of student departure require a scholarship of practice that embraces two purposes: the improvement of administrative practice in higher education and the development of a knowledge base befitting administrative work (Braxton, 2005). A scholarship of practice can emerge around a wide variety of administrative roles and functions (Braxton, 2005). In this case, a scholarship of practice centers on actions to increase institutional rates of student persistence. The need for such a scholarship of practice emanates from the inability of most colleges and universities to translate their knowledge and understanding of college student retention into actions that result in substantial gains in student retention and graduation (Tinto, 2006).

The empirical research described in the previous chapters of this volume contributes to both purposes of a scholarship of practice by generating replicative and applicatory knowledge, two forms of knowledge used in professional practice. Replicative knowledge pertains to knowledge needed to guide routines of professional practice, and applicatory knowledge entails the translation of technical knowledge into forms amenable for institutional action (Eraut, 1988). The staffing of introductory courses constitutes one administrative routine that benefits from empirical research reported in this volume. Moreover, the knowledge provided by the configuration of findings described in the previous chapters provides technical knowledge translatable into prescriptions for institutional action, designed to increase institutional rates of student retention. In this case, the applicatory knowledge that

NEW DIRECTIONS FOR TEACHING AND LEARNING, no. 115, Fall 2008 © Wiley Periodicals, Inc.
Published online in Wiley InterScience (www.interscience.wiley.com) • DOI: 10.1002/tl.328

emerges involves aspects of the college classroom such as curricular arrangements and teaching practices as levers for institutional action.

Contributions to a Scholarship of Practice Centered on Student Retention

The patterns of findings that emerge from the empirical research reported in the previous chapters make three significant contributions to a scholarship of practice centered on improving institutional rates of student retention. One of these contributions pertains to replicative knowledge, and the other two relate to applicatory knowledge.

Replicative Knowledge and Instructional Staffing of Gatekeeper Courses. Instructional course staffing assignments constitute a routine of academic administrative practice. Gatekeeper courses present challenges to academic administrative practice faced with staffing a large number of sections and limited financial resources to appoint additional full-time faculty to staff such courses. Tobias (1992) defines gatekeeper courses as introductory courses required for matriculation into a major field of study; they typically have high enrollments. Instructional staffing of such courses requires replicative knowledge because the instructional choices include full-time tenured and tenure-track faculty members, graduate students, and part-time instructors. The findings of Eagan and Jaeger (Chapter Three) indicate that staffing gatekeeper courses with graduate students wields little or no influence on student departure. However, staffing them with part-time faculty contributes to student departure. Such part-time instructors include adjunct professors, part-time lecturers, and postdoctoral researchers. The findings of Eagan and Jaeger reinforce those of Ehrenberg and Zhang (2005), who also found that increments in the number of part-time faculty to staff courses negatively affect student retention.

These findings strongly indicate that colleges and universities should avoid staffing gatekeeper courses with part-time faculty members such as part-time adjuncts, part-time lecturers, and postdoctoral researchers. Thus, the findings of Eagan and Jaeger, coupled with those of Ehrenberg and Zhang (2005), make a contribution to the scholarship of practice in general and replicative knowledge in particular.

Contributions to Applicatory Knowledge. The configuration of findings of the previous chapters also makes two contributions to a scholarship of practice centered on improving institutional rates of student retention by providing applicatory knowledge. The first pertains to the role of the college classroom in fostering multiple forms of student success. The attainment of some degree of confidence in the influence of faculty use of active learning in the retention of students constitutes the second contribution.

Fostering Multiple Forms of Student Success. Tinto (2006) contends that college and university faculty members do not view student retention as their responsibility. However, institutional interests in increasing student retention arise from the negative effects of student departure on the stability of institutional enrollments, budgets, and the public perception of the quality of colleges and universities (Braxton, Hirschy, and McClendon, 2004). Thus, college and university faculty members view institutional efforts to increase institutional rates of student retention as an administrative matter. Put differently, faculty members tend to view such institutional efforts as seeking an instrumental goal and not a substantive goal such as enhancing student learning. As a consequence, they disregard student retention as their responsibility. However, a knowledge and understanding of the role various aspects of the college classroom play in fostering multiple forms of student success may persuade faculty members to embrace student retention as one of their responsibilities because to do so also has a positive impact on student course learning.

To elaborate, students experience success in college in multiple ways, as eight domains of such success exist: academic attainment, acquisition of general education, development of academic competence, development of cognitive skills and intellectual dispositions, occupational attainment, preparation for adulthood and citizenship, personal accomplishments, and personal development (Braxton, 2006). Student course-level learning constitutes a fundamental contributor to the attainment of six of these eight domains of student success: academic attainment, acquisition of general education, development of academic competence, development of cognitive skills and intellectual dispositions, occupational attainment, and preparation for adulthood and citizenship. The achievement of specific markers of student success within each of these six domains depends on course content; nevertheless, student course-level learning continues as the foremost contributor. However, student course learning plays, at best, an indirect role in the attainment of student success associated with the domains of personal accomplishments and personal development (Braxton, 2006).

The contribution of student course-level learning to the six domains of student success becomes more evident through a brief description of specific indicators of success within each of these six domains. For example, academic attainment includes such indicators as year-to-year persistence, graduation, and academic learning (Braxton, 2006). The acquisition of general education consists of such indicators as the acquisition of a general knowledge of arts and sciences, learning about significant cultures of the world, and knowledge of community and world problems. The domain of the development of academic competence involves such specific markers of success as writing and speaking in a clear and effective manner, reading and mathematical skills, and meeting the requirements of a major. The development of cognitive skills and intellectual dispositions includes such markers as critical thinking, problem-solving skills, and the development of intellectual interests. Specific indicators of success in the domain of occupational attainment include obtaining employment after graduation in the same field as one's major and experiencing job satisfaction. The domain of

New Directions for Teaching and Learning • DOI: 10.1002/tl

preparation for adulthood and citizenship consists of such specific indicators of success as the presentation of one's self and one's ideas in an accept-
able manner, learning how to lead a group, and knowledge of government
(Braxton, 2006).

Pedagogical practices, course assessment procedures, and Chickering and
Gamson's principles of good practice (1987) for undergraduate education constitute aspects of faculty classroom teaching role performance that contribute
to student course level learning (Braxton, 2008). Pedagogical practices
include faculty teaching skills as well as methods of teaching. Course assessment procedures that enhance student course learning place an emphasis on
higher-order thinking skills such as analysis and synthesis of course content.
Teaching skills that contribute to student course learning include organization
and preparation and instructional clarity (Pascarella and others, 1996; Hines,
Cruickshank, and Kennedy, 1985; Schonwetter, Menec, and Perry, 1995;
Schonwetter, Perry, and Struthers, 1994; Wood and Murray, 1999). These
teaching skills also play a role in college student retention. The findings of
Pascarella, Seifert and Whitt reported in Chapter Four provide some evidence
of the positive role these teaching skills play in college student retention.
Their findings corroborate the findings of Braxton, Bray, and Berger (2000).

Moreover, active learning constitutes a method of teaching that
enhances student course learning and positively influences college student
retention. "Any class activity that "involves students in doing things and
thinking about things they are doing" makes up active learning (Bonwell
and Eison, 1991, p. 2). Empirical research exhibits the influence of active
learning on student course learning (Pascarella and Terenzini, 2005; Anderson and Adams, 1992; Chickering and Gamson, 1987; Johnson, Johnson,
and Smith, 1991; McKeachie, Pintrich, Yi Guang, and Smith, 1986). Moreover, the findings of several of the chapters of this volume also indicate that
faculty who use active learning in their courses have a positive impact on
college student retention. More specifically, the findings described by
Engstrom in Chapter One; Kinzie, Gonyea, Shoup, and Kuh in Chapter Two;
Braxton, Jones, Hirschy, and Hartley in Chapter Five; and Nelson Laird,
Chen, and Kuh in Chapter Six provide empirical support for this assertion.
Moreover, as we learn from Chapters One and Six, active learning enhances
the persistence of under-prepared students.

Course assessment procedures that enhance student course learning
accentuate higher-order thinking skills such as analysis and synthesis of
course content (Braxton, 2008; Renaud and Murray, 2007). In Chapter Six,
Laird, Chen, and Kuh report that academic challenge plays a positive role
in college student retention. The emphasis a course places on such higher-
order thinking skills as analysis and synthesis forms a critical aspect of the
notion of academic challenge.

Chickering and Gamson (1987) identify principles of good practice for
undergraduate education. Faculty adherence to these principles positively
influences student learning, as evidenced by a robust body of research (Sor-

cinelli, 1991). Such principles of good practice as encouragement of student and faculty contact, communication of high expectations, and respect for diverse talents and ways of knowing correspond to teaching practices that also have a positive effect on college student persistence.

The encouragement of student and faculty contact entails frequent interaction between students both in and out of the classroom (Chickering and Gamson, 1987). In Chapter Six, Laird, Chen, and Kuh offer some empirical evidence that student and faculty interactions play a positive role in college student retention.

The communication of high expectations involves not only setting high expectations for students but also expecting them to meet them (Chickering and Gamson, 1987). In Chapter One, Engstrom identifies student validation as a teaching practice used by faculty members in learning communities that plays a beneficial role in the retention of underprepared students enrolled in community colleges. Student validation parallels the Chickering and Gamson's principle of good practice labeled "communication of high expectations." To elaborate, Engstrom describes the validation of students as faculty setting high expectations for students and assuring them that they are capable of doing college work.

Student validation also involves the recognition faculty members give to the expertise and knowledge of students. Thus, this aspect of the teaching practice of student validation corresponds to Chickering and Gamson's good practice of demonstrating respect for diverse talents and ways of knowing.

To sum up, the pedagogical practices of active learning, the teaching skills of instructional clarity, course assessment practices that emphasize higher-order thinking skills, and Chickering and Gamson's principles of good practice in undergraduate education in the form of encouraging student and faculty contact, communication of high expectations, and respecting diverse talents and ways of knowing contribute to multiple forms of student success through their positive impact on college student retention and student course-level learning.

Toward Confidence. A scholarship of practice focused on the development and refinement of applicatory knowledge benefits from reliable knowledge (Braxton, 2005), which obtains from replication of research findings across different studies. A scholarship of practice centered on improving institutional rates of student retention gains some degree of confidence from reasonably reliable or consistent research findings, findings used to develop polices and practices for institutional action.

The role that faculty use of active learning in their courses plays in college student retention edges toward consistency, as evidenced by the findings reported in four of the chapters of this volume: Engtrom in Chapter One; Kinzie, Kinzie, Gonyea, Shoup, and Kuh in Chapter Two; Braxton, Jones, Hirschy, and Hartley in Chapter Five; and Laird, Chen, and Kuh in Chapter Six. The findings of these chapters join those of Braxton, Milem, and Sullivan (2000). Thus, five studies conducted in different institutional settings suggest a positive role for active learning in student retention.

Braxton and Lee (2005) used a threshold of ten or more studies that focused on a particular factor. To be judged as reliable, 70 percent of these studies must yield affirming results. Such a standard implies a high degree of reliability or consistency in results. However, Braxton and Lee (2005) recognize that some individuals may desire a different threshold and percentage of consistent results. When Braxton and Lee's criterion is used as a benchmark, five confirming studies suggest a moderate degree of consistency or reliability in findings. Such a degree of consistency provides some measure of assurance in the efficacy of institutional policies and activities that stress faculty use of active learning to increase institutional rates of student retention. With further replication, the role of faculty teaching skills may also attain a moderate degree of reliability.

Motivating College and University Faculty Members

The above two contributions to applicatory knowledge centered on improving institutional rates of college student retention strongly indicate a need for policies and practices designed to motivate college and university faculty members to make professional choices in their teaching that entail the acquisition of the teaching skills of instructor clarity and organization/preparation, the use of active learning, the use of course assessment procedures that enhance student course learning and accentuate higher-order thinking skills, and the application of such principles of good practice in undergraduate education as encouraging student and faculty contact, communication of high expectations, and respect for diverse talents and ways of knowing (Chickering and Gamson, 1987). These teaching choices contribute not only to student persistence but also to the more fundamental goal of student course-level learning.

College and university faculty members are free to make professional choices in their teaching because of the considerable autonomy they hold in their teaching role performance (Braxton and Bayer, 1999). Moreover, the choice of college and university faculty members to acquire the teaching skills of instructor clarity and organization/preparation, the use of active learning, the use of course assessment procedures that enhance student course learning that accentuate higher-order thinking skills, and the application of such principles of good practice in undergraduate education as encouraging student and faculty contact, communication of high expectations, and respecting diverse talents and ways requires some degree of effort by faculty members to engage in these teaching practices. Lecturing predominates, given that more than three-fourths (76.2 percent) of college and university faculty members use it as their primary method of instruction (Finkelstein, Seal, and Schuster, 1998). Thus, the choice of faculty to engage in teaching practices that go beyond lecturing requires some expenditure of effort by college and university faculty members.

The tenets of a theory of professional choices in teaching postulates that clear expectations for teaching role performance communicated by the central administration of a college or university and department chairpersons constitute a necessary but not a sufficient condition to motivate faculty members to engage in teaching practices that require some effort to enact (Braxton, 2008). To motivate most faculty members to expend the effort necessary to enact such teaching practices, individual college and university faculty members must perceive that they will receive such valued extrinsic rewards as tenure, promotion, continued appointment, and increases in annual salary as a result of their expended effort (Braxton, 2008). Nevertheless, some faculty members will be motivated to make such teaching choices without the expectancy of such extrinsic rewards.

A set of recommendations for institutional policy and practice springs from these formulations. These recommendations represent modifications of previous recommendations advanced by Braxton (2006) to motivate faculty members to make professional choices in teaching that foster student success:

- The president, chief academic affairs officer, and academic deans of colleges and universities desiring faculty teaching role performance directed toward increasing student retention and improving student course learning should publicly express their commitment and support for such efforts (Braxton, 2006). Public speeches, speeches made before university assemblies, memoranda, and the day-to-day conversations of members of the central administration should express such an institutional commitment. Such expression by members of the central administration imparts the clear institutional expectation that the faculty should make professional choices in their teaching that contribute to student course learning and student retention.
- Centers for teaching and faculty development programs should offer workshops or seminars on such topics as instructional clarity, active learning, higher-order thinking skills in course assessments, and such principles of good practice in undergraduate education as the encouragement of student and faculty contact, setting high expectations, and respecting diverse talents and ways of knowing. As an outcome of participation in such workshops and seminars, faculty members will perceive that they have the requisite knowledge of these teaching practices to expend the effort needed to enact these various teaching practices.
- Student course rating instruments should include items that gauge faculty engagement in those aspects of teaching role performance that contribute to student retention and other forms of college student success. Specifically, items should index the teaching skills of instructional clarity and organization/preparation, active learning, use of course assessment procedures that enhance student course learning and accentuate higher-order

thinking skills, and the application of such principles of good practice in undergraduate education as encouraging student and faculty contact, communication of high expectations, and respecting diverse talents and ways of knowing. The inclusion of such items on student course rating instruments communicates a clear message about institutional expectations for faculty to make professional choices of these teaching practices. Moreover, student ratings on these items can be used in making such faculty personnel decisions as tenure, promotion, reappointment, and annual salary increases.

- The academic reward structures of colleges and universities should allocate some weight to above-average faculty performance of such aspects of teaching as the teaching skills of instructional clarity and organization/preparation, the use of active learning, the use of course assessment procedures that enhance student course learning and accentuate higher-order thinking skills, and the application of such principles of good practice in undergraduate education as encouraging student and faculty contact, communication of high expectations, and respecting diverse talents and ways of knowing. Put differently, individual faculty members who expend effort to enact the aspects of teaching role performance that contribute to student learning and student retention should perceive that they will receive such valued outcomes for their efforts as an increase in annual salary, tenure, promotion, or reappointment.

These recommendations should augment other institutional efforts designed to improve institutional rates of student retention; many small institutional practices and activities designed to increase student retention rather than one major institutional practice should be developed and implemented (Braxton, Hirschy, and McClendon, 2004). This recommendation stems from Pascarella and Terenzini's advice (1991) on the need for multiple policy levers to effect change in students. As the chapters of this volume demonstrate, the college classroom plays a significant part in student retention. However, other factors also foster or impede student retention. Theory suggests that organizational characteristics play an important role in both commuter and residential institutions of higher education (Braxton, Hirschy, and McClendon, 2004). In residential institutions, the social communities contribute in a significant way, whereas the external environment exerts a strong influence on student departure in commuter colleges and universities (Braxton, Hirschy, and McClendon, 2004). Thus, these recommendations should not supplant other institutional policies and practices formulated to improve institutional rates of student retention.

The effectiveness of these recommendations in motivating faculty members to engage in teaching practices that foster student retention and student learning may vary by institutional type, academic discipline, and various faculty characteristics. The missions of colleges and universities shape institutional structures (Ruscio, 1987). Institutional structures in turn affect

NEW DIRECTIONS FOR TEACHING AND LEARNING • DOI: 10.1002/tl

academic work (Blackburn and Lawrence, 1995; Ruscio, 1987). As a consequence, greater success may obtain in teaching-oriented colleges and universities than in research-oriented universities. However, differences in success between residential and commuter colleges and universities appear unlikely given the postulated role of the classroom in both types of institutions (Braxton, Hirschy, and McClendon, 2004).

The faculty member's academic discipline may also moderate the effectiveness of the recommendations presented here. Academic disciplines vary in their level of paradigmatic development, that is, the level of consensus in an academic discipline on such matters as theoretical orientation, appropriateness of research methods, and the importance of various problems (Kuhn, 1962, 1970; Lodahl and Gordon, 1972; Biglan, 1973). Paradigmatic development and consensus are interchangeable descriptors of academic disciplines (Braxton and Hargens, 1996). Research demonstrates differences in teaching between faculty in high- and low-consensus disciplines. Physics and chemistry are examples of high-consensus disciplines, whereas political science and sociology are examples of low-consensus academic subject matter areas (Biglan, 1973). Faculty in low-consensus disciplines express a greater interest in teaching and receive higher student course evaluations than faculty members in high-consensus fields (Braxton and Hargens, 1996). Moreover, faculty members in low-consensus disciplines tend to display more of an affinity for efforts to improve undergraduate education than faculty members in high-consensus fields (Braxton, Olsen, and Simmons, 1998; Braxton, 1995). Given this pattern of findings, faculty members in low-consensus fields may exhibit greater motivation to perform teaching practices that facilitate student retention and student learning than faculty members holding membership in high-consensus fields. As a consequence, the four recommendations presented in this chapter may wield a greater influence on faculty members in low-consensus disciplines than on academics in high-consensus fields.

Gender and tenure status constitute faculty characteristics that may govern the effectiveness of these four recommendations. Women faculty members express a greater commitment to teaching than do male faculty members (Bayer and Astin, 1975; Boyer, 1990; Boice, 1992; Tierney and Rhoads, 1993). Thus, these recommendations may display a greater degree of efficacy for women academics than for male faculty members. Because untenured faculty members view good teaching as "good content" (Paulsen and Feldman, 1995), these recommendations may exert less of an influence on untenured faculty than on tenured faculty members.

Concluding Thoughts

As indicated in the Editor's Notes and at the beginning of this chapter, Tinto (2006) laments the problems that colleges and universities face in translating theory and research into forms of action that lead to success. However, this chapter and the others in this volume provide support for a scholarship

New Directions for Teaching and Learning • DOI: 10.1002/tl

of practice focused on the translation of research findings into recommendations for policy and practice designed to increase institutional rates of student retention.

The configuration of findings reported here, coupled with the formulations of this chapter, also supply strong support for Tinto's assertion that the classroom occupies fertile ground for the translation of theory and research into practice. As the formulations of this chapter suggest, the key to gaining faculty acceptance of the important function of the classroom in student retention lies in the influence various teaching practices wield on student retention and other forms of college student success, especially those involving student course learning. As suggested by the four recommendations advanced in this chapter, the central administration of colleges and universities, centers for teaching and faculty development bear a substantial responsibility for gaining such essential faculty acceptance of the role of the classroom in improving institutional rates of student retention.

References

Anderson, J. A., and Adams, A. M. "Acknowledging the Learning Styles of Diverse Student Populations: Implications for Instructional Design." In L.L.B. Border and V. N. Chism (eds.), *Teaching for Diversity*. New Directions for Teaching and Learning, no. 49. San Francisco: Jossey-Bass, 1992.

Bayer, A. E., and Astin, H. S. "Sex Differentials in the Academic Reward System." *Science*, 1975, *188*, 796–802.

Biglan, A. "The Characteristics of Subject Matter in Different Academic Areas." *Journal of Applied Psychology*, 1973, *57*(3), 195–203.

Blackburn, R. T., and Lawrence, J. H. *Faculty at Work: Motivation, Expectation, Satisfaction*. Baltimore, Md.: Johns Hopkins University Press. 1995.

Boice, R. *The New Faculty Member: Supporting and Fostering Professional Development*. San Francisco: Jossey-Bass, 1992.

Bonwell, C. C., and Eison, J. A. *Active Learning: Creating Excitement in the Classroom*. ASHE-ERIC Higher Education Report, no. 1. San Francisco: Jossey-Bass, 1991.

Boyer, E. L. *Scholarship Reconsidered: Priorities of the Professoriate*. Stanford, Calif.: Carnegie Foundation for the Advancement of Teaching, 1990.

Braxton, J. M. "Disciplines with an Affinity for the Improvement of Undergraduate Education." In N. Hativa and M. Marincovich (eds.), *Disciplinary Differences in Teaching and Learning: Implications for Practice*. San Francisco: Jossey-Bass, 1995.

Braxton, J. M. "Reflections on a Scholarship of Practice." *Review of Higher Education*, 2005, *28*(2), 285–293.

Braxton, J. M. *Faculty Professional Choices in Teaching That Foster Student Success*. Washington, D.C.: National Postsecondary Education Cooperative, 2006.

Braxton, J. M. "Toward a Theory of Faculty Professional Choice in Teaching That Fosters College Student Success." In J. C. Smart (ed.), *Higher Education: Handbook of Theory and Research* (vol. 23, pp. 181–207). Dordrecht: Springer, 2008.

Braxton, J. M., and Bayer, A. E. *Faculty Misconduct in Collegiate Teaching*. Baltimore, Md.: Johns Hopkins University Press, 1999.

Braxton, J. M., Bray, N. J., and Berger, J. B. "Faculty Teaching Skills and Their Influence on the College Student Departure Process." *Journal of College Student Development*, 2000, *41*(2), 215–227.

Braxton, J. M., and Hargens, L. L. "Variations Among Academic Disciplines: Analytical Frameworks and Research." In J. C. Smart (ed.), *Higher Education: Handbook of Theory and Research*. New York: Agathon Press, 1996.

Braxton, J. M., Hirschy, A. S., and McClendon, S. A. *Toward Understanding and Reducing College Student Departure*. ASHE-ERIC Higher Education Report, vol. 30, no. 3. San Francisco: Jossey-Bass, 2004.

Braxton, J. M., and Lee, S. D. "Toward Reliable Knowledge About College Student Departure." In A. Seidman (ed.), *College Student Retention: Formula for Success*. Westport, Conn.: American Council on Higher Education/Praeger, 2005.

Braxton, J. M., and Lien, L. A. "The Viability of Academic Integration as a Central Construct in Tinto's Interactionalist Theory of College Student Departure." In Braxton, J. M., Milem, J. F., and Sullivan, A. S. "The Influence of Active Learning on the College Student Departure Process: Toward a Revision of Tinto's Theory." *Journal of Higher Education*, 2000, *71*(5), 569–590.

Braxton, J. M., Olsen, D., and Simmons, A. "Affinity Disciplines and the Use of Principles of Good Practice for Undergraduate Education." *Research in Higher Education*, 1998, *39*, 299–318.

Chickering, A. W., and Gamson, Z. F. "Seven Principles for Good Practice." *AAHE Bulletin*, 1987, *39*, 3–7.

Ehrenberg, R. G., and Zhang, L. "Do Tenure and Tenure-Track Faculty Matter?" *Journal of Human Resources*, 2005, *40*, 647–659.

Eraut, M. "Knowledge Creation and Knowledge Use in Professional Contexts." *Studies in Higher Education*, 1988, *10*, 117–132.

Finkelstein, M. J., Seal, R. K., and Schuster, J. H. *The New Academic Generation: A Profession in Transition*. Baltimore, Md.: Johns Hopkins University Press, 1998.

Hines, C. V., Cruickshank, D. R., and Kennedy, J. J. "Teacher Clarity and Its Relationship to Student Achievement and Satisfaction." *American Educational Research Journal*, 1985, *22*, 87–99.

Johnson, D. W., Johnson, R. T., and Smith, K. A. *Cooperative Learning: Increasing College Faculty Instructional Productivity*. ASHE-ERIC Higher Education Report, no. 4. San Francisco: Jossey-Bass, 1991.

Kuhn, T. S. *The Structure of Scientific Revolutions*. Chicago: University of Chicago Press, 1972.

Lodahl, J. B., and Gordon, G. G. "The Structure of Scientific Fields and the Functioning of University Graduate Departments." *American Sociological Review*, 1972, *37*(1), 57–72.

McKeachie, W. J., Pintrich, P. R., Yi-Guang, L., and Smith, D.A.F. *Teaching and Learning in the College Classroom: A Review of the Research Literature*. Ann Arbor: Regents of the University of Michigan, 1986.

Pascarella, E. T., and Terenzini, P. T. *How College Affects Students*. San Francisco: Jossey-Bass, 1991.

Pascarella, E. T., and Terenzini, P. T. *How College Affects Students*, Vol. 2: *A Third Decade of Research*. San Francisco: Jossey-Bass, 2005.

Pascarella, E., and others. "Effects of Teacher Organization/Preparation and Teacher Skill/Clarity on General Cognitive Skills in College." *Journal of College Student Development*, 1996, *37*, 7–19.

Paulsen, M. B., and Feldman, K. A. *Taking Teaching Seriously: Meeting the Challenge of Instructional Improvement*. ASHE-ERIC Higher Education Report, no. 2. San Francisco: Jossey-Bass, 1995.

Renaud, R. D., and Murray, H. G. "The Validity of Higher-Order Questions as a Process Indicator of Educational Quality." *Research in Higher Education*, 2007, *48*, 319–351.

Ruscio, K. P. "Many Sectors, Many Professions." In B. R. Clark (ed.), *The Academic Profession*. Berkeley: University of California Press, 1987.

Schonwetter, D., Menec, V., and Perry, R. "An Empirical Comparison of Two Effective College Teaching Behaviors: Expressiveness and Organization." Paper presented at the annual meeting of the American Educational Research Association, San Francisco, Apr. 1995.

Schonwetter, D., Perry, R. P., and Struthers, C. W. "Students' Perceptions of Control and Success in the College Classroom: Affects and Achievement in Different Instructional Conditions." *Journal of Experimental Education,* 1994, *61,* 227–246.

Sorcinelli, M. D. ""Research Findings on the Seven Principles." In A. W. Chickering and Z. F. Gamson (eds.), *Applying the Seven Principles of Good Practice in Undergraduate Education.* San Francisco: Jossey-Bass, 1991.

Tierney, W. G., and Rhoads, R. A. *Enhancing Promotion, Tenure and Beyond: Faculty Socialization as a Cultural Process.* ASHE-ERIC Report, no. 6. San Francisco: Jossey-Bass,, 1993.

Tinto, V. "Research and Practice of Student Retention: What Next?" *Journal of College Student Retention,* 2006, *8*(1), 1–19.

Tobias, S. "Science Education Reform: What's Wrong with the Process?" In S. Tobias (ed.), *Revitalizing Undergraduate Science: Why Some Things Works and Most Don't.* Tucson, Ariz.: Research Corporation, 1992.

Wood, A., and Murray, H. "Effects of Teacher Enthusiasm on Student Attention, Motivation, and Memory Encoding." Paper presented at the annual meeting of the American Educational Research Association, Montreal, Canada, Apr. 1999.

JOHN M. BRAXTON *is professor of education in the Higher Education Leadership and Policy Program at Peabody College, Vanderbilt University, in Nashville, Tennessee.*

INDEX

NEW DIRECTIONS FOR TEACHING AND LEARNING
Order Form
SUBSCRIPTIONS AND SINGLE ISSUES

DISCOUNTED BACK ISSUES:

Use this form to receive **20% off** all back issues of New Directions for
Teaching and Learning. All single issues priced at **$23.20** (normally $29.00).

TITLE	ISSUE NO.	ISBN
_____	_____	_____
_____	_____	_____
_____	_____	_____

Call 888-378-2537 or see mailing instructions below. When calling, mention the
promotional code, JB7ND, to receive your discount.

SUBSCRIPTIONS: *(1 year, 4 issues)*

☐ New Order   ☐ Renewal

U.S.	☐ Individual: $80	☐ Institutional: $195
Canada/Mexico	☐ Individual: $80	☐ Institutional: $235
All Others	☐ Individual: $104	☐ Institutional: $269

Call 888-378-2537 or see mailing and pricing instructions below. Online
subscriptions are available at www.interscience.wiley.com.

Copy or detach page and send to:
John Wiley & Sons, Journals Dept, 5th Floor
989 Market Street, San Francisco, CA 94103-1741

Order Form can also be faxed to: 888-481-2665

Issue/Subscription Amount: $ _____
Shipping Amount: $ _____
(for single issues only—subscription prices include shipping)
Total Amount: $ _____

SHIPPING CHARGES:

SURFACE	Domestic	Canadian
First Item	$5.00	$6.00
Each Add'l Item	$3.00	$1.50

(No sales tax for U.S. subscriptions. Canadian residents, add GST for subscription orders. Individual rate subscriptions
must be paid by personal check or credit card. Individual rate subscriptions may not be resold as library copies.)

☐ Payment enclosed (U.S. check or money order only. All payments must be in U.S. dollars.)

☐ VISA ☐ MC ☐ Amex # _____ Exp. Date_____

Card Holder Name _____ Card Issue # _____

Signature_____ Day Phone _____

☐ Bill Me (U.S. institutional orders only. Purchase order required.)

Purchase order # _____
Federal Tax ID13559302   GST 89102 8052

Name_____

Address _____

Phone _____ E-mail _____

JB7ND

Complete online access for your institution

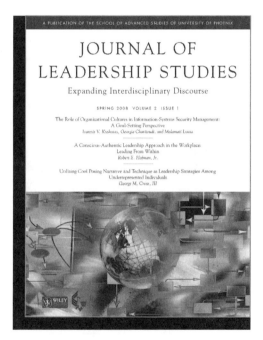

A PUBLICATION OF THE SCHOOL OF ADVANCED STUDIES OF UNIVERSITY OF PHOENIX

JOURNAL OF LEADERSHIP STUDIES

Expanding Interdisciplinary Discourse

SPRING 2008   VOLUME 2   ISSUE 1

The Role of Organizational Cultures in Information-Systems Security Management:
A Goal-Setting Perspective
Ioannis V. Koskosas, Georgia Charitoudi, and Malamati Louta

A Conscious-Authentic Leadership Approach in the Workplace:
Leading From Within
Robert E. Hofman, Jr.

Utilizing Cool Posing Narrative and Technique as Leadership Strategies Among
Underrepresented Individuals
George M. Cross, III

Register for complimentary online access to *Journal of Leadership Studies* today!

Why Wait to Make Great Discoveries

When you can make them in an instant with Wiley InterScience® Pay-Per-View and ArticleSelect™

Now you can have instant, full-text access to an extensive collection of journal articles or book chapters available on Wiley InterScience. With Pay-Per-View and ArticleSelect™, there's no limit to what you can discover...

ArticleSelect™ is a token-based service, providing access to full-text content from non-subscribed journals to existing institutional customers (EAL and BAL)

Pay-per-view is available to any user, regardless of whether they hold a subscription with Wiley InterScience.

Benefits:

• Access online full-text content from journals and books that are outside your current library holdings

• Use it at home, on the road, from anywhere at any time

• Build an archive of articles and chapters targeted for your unique research needs

• Take advantage of our free profiled alerting service the perfect companion to help you find specific articles in your field as soon as they're published

• Get what you need instantly no waiting for document delivery

• Fast, easy, and secure online credit card processing for pay-per-view downloads

• Special, cost-savings for EAL customers: whenever a customer spends tokens on a title equaling 115% of its subscription price, the customer is auto-subscribed for the year

• Access is instant and available for 24 hours

⊛WILEY
InterScience®
DISCOVER SOMETHING GREAT

www.interscience.wiley.com

4760

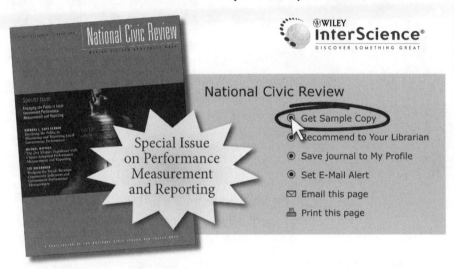